The Twelve Step Journal

The Twelve Step *Journal*

Claudette Wassil-Grimm, M. Ed.

THE OVERLOOK PRESS
WOODSTOCK • NEW YORK

First published in 1996 by
The Overlook Press
Lewis Hollow Road
Woodstock, New York 12498

Library of Congress Cataloging-in-Publication Data

Wassil-Grimm, Claudette.
The twelve-step journal / Claudette Wassil-Grimm.
p. cm.
1. Alcoholics—Rehabilitation. 2. Twelve-step programs.
3. Workaholics—Rehabilitation. 4. Addicts—Rehabilitation
I. Title
HV5275.W35 1995 616.86′106--dc20 95-18049
ISBN 0-87951-618-6

1 3 5 7 9 10 8 6 4 2
First Edition
Manufactured in the United States of America

To Meredith

CONTENTS

Acknowledgments

First of all I would like to thank all the readers who reviewed the book "in progress" and added suggestions that improved the manuscript tremendously. High on this list are David E. Adams, Kathi Bedard, Marvin Berman, Anita Lampel, and Anna Marcel de Hermanas. Other readers who offered much appreciated support during the project are Dudley Atherton, Bill Bennett, Alan F. Carney, Jim Christopher, Lynn Ellis, Jim Haueter, Melody Haueter, Ruth Hollman, Coleen M. Salhaney, Tom Shelley, Jack Trimpey, Don W., and the members of the Athens SOS group.

Special thanks go to my assistant Maureen Olander, and to my husband Andy and my son Jerzy for their patience when I was inaccessible.

The Twelve Step *Journal*

INTRODUCTION

I HAVE KEPT A JOURNAL since I quit drinking and using twenty-two years ago. At that time, I discovered that it helped me clarify my thoughts. Without a journal I seemed to have insights and then promptly lose them. The very act of writing down my insights fixed them more clearly in my memory. I felt that I was finally moving forward rather than running in circles.

Keeping a journal can help you on your journey to recovery in many ways. Right now, your life is on the verge of great change. An old era is ending and a new one is beginning. Your new life will require many changes. For example, you must make decisions about how you will now spend the time you used to devote to your addiction. The decisions you make about how to spend that time will affect the quality of your life in your next "stage."

One good way to spend some of this time is to keep a journal. It is best to establish a journal writing routine and stick to it. Most prefer to write a little in their journals every day, when they wake up or right before bed. You might choose to write at the time when you would have indulged in your addiction (like right after work) or you may be rearranging your entire schedule in some way that you feel will most help you resist returning to your addiction. One suggestion is to add journal writing and Twelve Step meetings to your calendar at "cocktail hour." If you spent ten hours a week at a bar or drinking with friends, then you should now have at least ten hours available for meetings and journal writing.

Set yourself up in a comfortable place, perhaps with a cup of hot decaf coffee or herbal tea, or in the summers, a cold soda or lemonade. The minimum time you should spend on your journal is twenty minutes a day or two hours a week in one large block, perhaps on a weekend morning. I recommend that you pace yourself so that you can complete one chapter; that is, one step, per month. That would carry you through that first challenging year.

Because this book is not a complete text to recovery, you will need to do some supplemental reading. Also, during the first few weeks or months of sobriety you may not be your sharpest. It should not surprise you if you take several weeks to do the first chapter and then find yourself gradually picking up speed. The beauty of a journal is that it is private and individually paced. You may take as much time as you need at any point.

By keeping a journal, we slow down and look at life more closely. Writing can be an important tool for thinking things through and capturing insights. When we look back through it, it provides a record of our changes and allows us to see that we are progressing. By keeping a journal regularly we begin to open ourselves to our "still small voice"[1] within and form the habit of listening to the wisest part of ourselves. Make a commitment to yourself to keep the journal at certain times, and then keep this commitment.

Diversity

Diversity has already become the watchword of the twenty-first century. Global economics, satellite communications, and jet travel have changed our world. America is no longer a melting pot; it's more like a fruit salad where each fruit retains its individual flavor. AA and other recovery programs have already been challenged by the need for diversity. An AA meeting might contain a drunk in remission, a former pothead, a mentally ill chemical abuser, an atheist, an agnostic, a Jew, a Muslim, a junkie struggling with AIDS, and a refugee from Nicaragua who does not yet speak English and believes he's at a citizenship class! How can one program meet the needs of all these people? Chances are it can't.

At the same time, some alcoholics, addicts, or overeaters may be in a remote area where there are no meetings to attend. There are as many different circumstances and needs that must be addressed as there are alcoholics and addicts. Even those who are

1. 1 Kings 19:12.

comfortable at meetings sometimes find that they are solitary learners and need to spend a great deal of time at home working alone on the Steps. Using a journal can help one gain perspective, sort through the appropriateness of other people's advice, and set priorities.

However, it is important to keep in mind the difference between *solitude* and *isolation*. Solitude is a positive choice.

Many people, especially introverts, find they think and sort more clearly when they are alone. As part of our recovery we should be listening to the advice of others, but we should only follow the advice that fits our situation and needs. We will inevitably hear contradictory advice or advice that does not apply to our situation at all and could backfire if we followed it. We need quiet time alone, thinking and journal writing, in order to be able to evaluate the new choices being presented to us. Jesus took forty days in the desert. Buddha sat under a tree to think. Reflection is as important as action.

On the other hand, the AA message about getting with a group can be so all-pervasive that we begin to fear being alone. As long as we are seeking solitude and not withdrawing from social contact out of fear, embarrassment, or excessive shyness—which we refuse to challenge—we need not worry. Some things are better done in a group, some things are not. Through experimentation you will gradually learn how much alone time you need and how much contact with other people you need. This is a very individual thing. If you are honest with yourself (and don't pretend to be seeking solitude when you are really withdrawing to brood), you will be able to trust your instincts in this area.

There are also many addicts who choose to follow the Twelve Steps in their own unique way. They have discovered that Twelve Step programs support and teach a way of life, a system of human values that can lead to feelings of greater harmony and self-control. However, many others have been driven off by aspects of the total Twelve Step package that they find uncomfortable. Indeed, in the case of alcoholics, studies show that 80 percent of all newcomers to AA drop out within the first thirty days, and 95 percent drop out within the first year. Some go on to a life of sobriety without AA, some return to drinking, and of these, some will later return to AA and stay. Though AA is highly effective for those who stick with it, there are many who do not stay long enough to benefit from Twelve Step programs.[2]

These are the two most frequently given reasons for abandoning the program:[3]

1. Some people cannot relate to the specific religious philosophy that is central to AA. In fact, some of those ordered to attend AA based treatment due to drunk driving and other alcohol-related violations feel their First Amendment rights are being violated.

2. Some people are uncomfortable with group situations and AA so strongly emphasizes the meetings that some newcomers don't believe they can benefit from the program without attending meetings constantly. Introverts may flee the program before they have found a way to make it work for them.

Most counselors who advise addicts now acknowledge that there are many paths to sobriety. Introverts may need to begin by seeking the counsel and support of a therapist who is well-informed about addictions and recovery. Not everyone can benefit from the "hard line" approach taken by many AAs. Phrases like "Take the cotton out of your ears and put it in your mouth," may feel hurtfully rude to some sensitive newcomers.

If you have had questions about whether AA or another Twelve Step organization is for you, you are not alone, and you are not doomed to failure. One study shows that 70 percent of those who recover from an addiction to alcohol do so without AA.[4] It is not only agnostics and atheists who resist AA, there are also some who wish to keep their religion and medical problems separate. Some regard their alcoholism as a health problem and believe that

---

2. Alcoholics Anonymous, *Alcoholics Anonymous 1989 Membership Survey* (New York: Alcoholics Anonymous World Services, 1990).

3. Jerry Dorsman, *How to Quit Drinking Without AA* (Rocklin, CA: Prima Publishing, 1994), p. 3.

4. S. Peele, *The Diseasing of America* (New York: Lexington Books, 1989) as quoted in *The Final Fix* by Jack Trimpey (Lotus, CA: Lotus Press, 1994), p. 12.

medical science may eventually find a medical cure for alcoholism. For example, a new drug called Naltrexone has been shown to lower the relapse rate for alcoholics to 23 percent.[5] How does this information fit in with a belief that only a higher power can take away our cravings?

The God Stuff

If you are a dissenter who has trouble with all "the God stuff," does this mean you cannot benefit from Twelve Step programs? Not necessarily. Many attend Twelve Step meetings even though they are agnostics or atheists. As Twelve Step spokespeople suggest, they "take what they like and leave the rest." Some find a definition of God, a Higher Power, or Greater Power[6] that is broad enough for them to live with. Most avoid arguing the point in meetings, but may go on taking the Twelve Steps without God. Though this works for some, many feel too alienated or hypocritical to continue.

AA meetings were vital to me the first year I quit drinking, yet I remember the painful feeling of isolation caused by my agnostic stance. I eventually developed a faith of my own but even then the Lord's Prayer, which is a Christian prayer, made me uncomfortable because I am not a Christian. Though Twelve Step groups can now vote to eliminate the Lord's Prayer and many simply use the Serenity Prayer, even the Serenity Prayer starts with the word "God."

Indeed, this has become a growing problem for those trying to fit in at meetings in the 1990s. Statistics show that 40 percent of people in the United States do not claim any religion. These are the agnostics, atheists, secularists, humanists, or nonbelievers. This is a very sizable

5. "Health Report," *Time,* (30 January, 1995), p. 20.

6. The phrase Greater Power, though not on the tip of everyone's tongue, is actually the most common term used in *The Big Book* to signify an alternative to the image of God, as the white-bearded man in the sky. "Greater Power" is used nine times in *The Big Book,* while "Higher Power" is only used twice. "Higher Power" has become the more popular term because of its use by Hazelden, a treatment center in Minnesota and publisher of Twelve Step literature. I will use the more unfamiliar term "Greater Power" because it carries fewer associations and connotations.

portion that may need special support while they are in the challenging transition of quitting an addiction.

Of the remaining 60 percent of the population, 93 percent are Christian. We tend to think we are being inclusive of all religions when we choose a prayer that is not specific to any Catholic or Protestant sect. However, in recent years more and more immigrants have come to the United States from non-European countries. Worldwide, Christianity is practiced by 33 percent of the world's people, but the next three largest groups—Muslims, Hindus, and Buddhists—make up 37 percent of the world's religious practice. As our culture becomes more diverse, we will need to pay more attention to these differences.

There are also those who do not want their faith in God to depend on their ability to remain sober. One woman explained that after five years of sobriety, she went on a binge when she began to have painful marital problems. She understands her behavior as a response to painful emotional stress and does not want to reframe the problem as either her lack of faith in God, or as God's failure to come through for her at a difficult time. Her need to separate God and sobriety would make her a maverick in AA.

Similarly one very religious man who chose Rational Recovery as his program explained,

> "I am a Christian. I believe that Jesus Christ is my personal Savior, and when I have a flat tire, I immediately get down on my knees. But, you see, I don't get on my knees to pray. It's to turn the lug wrench. When I pray, it's to worship, and not to ask for help with things that are *mine* to do—no matter how difficult."[7]

Of course, we do not want to throw out the baby with the bath water. As a recovery program, philosophy of life, or code of conduct, the Twelve Steps are very sound. They encourage the resolution of conflicts and injuries committed against and by others. This process allows those of us with addictions to put the past behind us and start fresh. The Twelve Steps teach much about how to treat other people

---

7. Quoted in Jack and Lois Trimpey, *Taming the Feast Beast* (New York: Delacorte Press, 1995), p. 115.

so that they will respond to us in positive ways. The Twelve Step programs also emphasize the ongoing need to resolve conflicts as they arise. These programs teach coping mechanisms that were either faulty or non-existent in the addict.

Another major benefit of Twelve Step programs is their ready availability. Chapters of AA, NA (Narcotics Anonymous), Al-Anon (for families), ACOA (for adult children of alcoholics), CODA (Codependents Anonymous), and OA (Overeaters Anonymous) are found in most large towns, and cities often offer an infinite variety of meetings, including smaller groups like Workaholics Anonymous. These groups strive to have a warm welcoming atmosphere and make a point of helping newcomers feel at home. Most people who try to quit a bad habit realize that it is easier if they avoid the company of others who share the habit. Twelve Step meetings offer a much-needed alternative to going to the bar or bakery.

Whether you are a Christian, atheist, agnostic, believe in Mohammed, are a practicing Jew, or prefer to keep your religion and recovery separate, this journal can help you stick out the early difficult stage of beginning a Twelve Step program. All the Steps are presented in their traditional form in the Appendix, but are restated in non theistic terms at the head of each step, so that those who are uncomfortable with Christian prayers or deistic imagery can see how the Step can be worked without reference to a "Greater Power." If this applies to you, know that while you work in your journal, there are thousands of others out there anonymously keeping you company.

Dual Diagnosis[8]

Another diverse category of addicts is the mentally ill addict. Recent research shows that about 40 percent of those with a major mental illness such as schizophrenia or bipolar disorder are also alcohol or chemical abusers. It has been AA policy in the past, and it is still the belief of many chemical dependency counselors, that a recovering addict should not be taking any kind of mood altering or psycho-

8. Katie Evans and J. Michael Sullivan, *Dual Diagnosis: Counseling the Mentally Ill Substance Abuser* (New York: Guilford Press, 1990).

tropic medication. This attitude stems from a destructive medical trend in the 1960s and 1970s, when many medical doctors prescribed Valium and other tranquilizers or sleep aids to alleviate the tension and anxiety that usually follow withdrawal. As a result, recovering addicts often became addicted to these new substances and fell back into their same self-destructive patterns.

However, modern medications for mood disorders and schizophrenia are not addictive and do not lead to relapse. Rather, they decrease depression, confusion, and poor functioning so that the recovering addict can maintain sobriety. AA World Services (the national headquarters) recognizes the benefits and necessity of these medications for dually diagnosed clients and has issued an official policy statement that those who need medication should not be discouraged from taking it. (Similarly, recovering addicts with a chronic physical illness such as cancer, Rheumatoid arthritis, or Krones disease are not discouraged from taking pain medication they may need, which are often similar to commonly abused drugs.) However, although AA can advise individual groups on national policy, they can not control what is said at each AA meeting.

Unfortunately, some AA meeting groups still chastise members for taking needed medication and do not consider members who take medication to be truly abstinent. Great pressure is sometimes applied to get mentally ill people to quit their prescribed medication and the results can be tragic. Without medication schizophrenics may have major mental breakdowns that require them to be hospitalized for months until they can be restabilized, and bipolar recovering addicts may become so severely depressed that they attempt suicide.

AA has tried to address this problem by offering Double Trouble meetings for dually diagnosed addicts. Most major cities offer such groups but less populated areas don't. Of the alternative programs, SOS (described below) is the only one that explicitly recognizes dual diagnosis addicts as a special subgroup. Because SOS emphasizes diversity and the need for each person's program to be designed to meet his or her individual needs, dual diagnosis addicts are welcomed and accepted in SOS.

Anxiety and Depression

By the time many addicts are ready to quit drinking or using destructively, they have probably gotten into the habit of escaping uncomfortable feelings by using their substance. The two most common and disturbingly intense feelings we desire to escape are anxiety[9] and depression.[10]

Many addicts have depended on their substance of choice for relaxation and know no other means of relaxing. Abstinence is therefore often accompanied by nervousness and anxiety. If they do not find new healthy ways to relax, their sobriety is likely to be compromised by this ever-present anxiety.

Anxious recovering addicts need to seek out and learn other methods of relaxation. In the workbook sections, I suggest some relaxation exercises. You will see that there are many different ways to relax and by experimentation you will learn what works for you. You might want to try listening to music or recordings of nature sounds; dancing, exercising, or yoga; meditation or progressive relaxation exercises; biofeedback, hydrotherapy, or massage; or reading absorbing books or watching movies. Try them all and save the best ones for your worst days when relapse threatens.

Many of these techniques can also break a depression, but sometimes depressives need something more active or engaging. They may need to get out among people they enjoy and actively engage in activities they like. Though many methods for relieving anxiety are successful when done alone, depressives should be wary of withdrawing from society and may do better reaching out to others for help in breaking their low moods.

Also keep in mind that if your depression or anxiety is severe and none of these proven methods provide much relief, you may have a dual diagnosis problem. People with anxiety disorders or depressive

---

9. A good book for anxiety is Claire Weekes, *Peace from Nervous Suffering* (New York: Signet, 1972).

10. For depression you may wish to read David D. Burns, *Feeling Good: The New Mood Therapy* (New York: NAL-Signet, 1981) or Mark S. Gold with Lois B. Morris, *The Good News About Depression: Cures and Treatments in the New Age of Psychiatry* (New York: Bantam Books, 1985).

disorders often turn to alcohol for relief. If they later quit drinking they will again re-experience the raw anxiety or depression. If this is the case, they may need to take corrective medication prescribed by a well-informed psychiatrist. Make sure anyone who prescribes medication for you is knowledgeable about both addictions and mental illnesses.

Alternative Programs

There are many groups springing up that practice healthy living principles (without making religious references) for those in recovery. You may find it helpful to look for or start your own non-theistic group. Three organizations, SOS, or Secular Organization for Sobriety (1,200 groups in the United States with 20,000 members), SMART Recovery, and RR, or Rational Recovery, emphasize recovery without religion and welcome people with other addictions. Within AA itself a group called Quad A (Alcoholics Anonymous for Atheists and Agnostics) is gaining momentum.[11]

SOS—This group is not anti-religious, they simply believe that alcoholism is a medical problem, not a spiritual one. SOS is secular—a nonreligious support group like the many shared-problem support groups for widows, cancer patients, AIDS victims, and so on. They reject AA because they feel that the Twelve Steps teach "learned helplessness," or reliance on God or groups rather than self-reliance. They acknowledge that though AA has helped countless thousands, it has not worked for thousands of others. There is room for alternative programs.

SOS believes in honoring diversity. Each individual comes to the group with a different set of needs, past experiences, and understandings. The SOS attitude about unresolved issues from the past is that

11. To find out if there is a group near you, or to start one of your own, contact:
Secular Organization for Sobriety, P.O. Box 5, Buffalo, N.Y., 14215-0005. 716/834-2922
SMART Recovery, 521 Mount Auburn St., Suite 200, Watertown, MA 02172. 617/891-7574.
Rational Recovery, Box 800, Lotus, CA, 95651. 916/621-2667
Quad A, Second Unitarian Church, 656 W. Barry Ave., Chicago, IL 60657

each SOS member has the personal option of choosing to work on behavior patterns they would like to change. They might choose to work with a therapist or to take courses for self-improvement. Members are supported in their positive efforts at change but no one tries to tell them what they should change. (See the appendix for the SOS principles.)

SOS is the only program that specifically mentions the problems of the dual diagnosis addict and is openly supportive of those who take properly prescribed medication.

SOS also looks to the future by focusing on sobriety as the first priority and then on building a new life with positive associations with sobriety living. Rather than focusing on "not drinking" (a negative), they focus on pleasurable sober living.

Its greatest popularity is in California where, since 1987, Los Angeles courts have given drunken drivers mandated to enter a program the option of attending either SOS or AA. Like AA, SOS holds meetings which serve as support groups, but unlike AA they do not have a sponsor system. They believe that sponsors can too easily become "gurus," and people should learn from a diversity of opinions.

SMART Recovery—SMART (Self-Management And Recovery Training) is an international, nonprofit organization that provides self-help for individuals who want to abstain from alcohol or other mood-altering substances. Based on the principles of Rational Emotive Behavior Therapy developed by Albert Ellis, SMART Recovery is different from AA in the following ways: 1) one need not declare oneself powerless, 2) one need not rely on "Greater Powers" to achieve and maintain abstinence, 3) one is not required to label oneself "alcoholic" or "addict," and 4) one need not spend the rest of one's life "in recovery" or going to meetings. SMART Recovery translates scientific research, particularly research in cognitive-behavioral psychology, into a self-help format.

This cognitive-behavioral approach can be summed up in these words of Epictetus, an ancient Greek philosopher who wrote, "People are disturbed not by things, but by the views they take of them." SMART Recovery aims to help participants change the distorted thoughts and beliefs that have led to their addictions. The program is regularly revised to keep up with new scientific research findings.

SMART Recovery emphasizes four main areas: 1) enhancing and maintaining motivation to change substance abusing or dependent behavior, 2) recognizing, but refusing to act on, urges or cravings to use substances, 3) encouraging ways to handle life problems other than by using substances, and 4) developing a positive, healthy lifestyle. It is assumed that participants attend meetings only until they are confident that they have made the changes in their thinking and behavior that will support their future sobriety. Breaking dependence on the recovery group is an expected part of the process of recovery from addiction, and one should continue to attend meetings after a dependable sobriety has been achieved only if he or she would enjoy helping others with their sobriety.

The groups are lead by coordinators who may or may not have once had an addiction problem that they solved by using the principles of SMART Recovery. All coordinators are well-versed in cognitive behavioral techniques and some are coordinators by virtue of their expertise, rather than their personal experience.

RR—Rational Recovery is also based on the Rational Emotive Behavior Therapy of Albert Ellis, a prolific writer and founder of this school of psychology. His book, *How to Refuse to Feel Bad About Anything, Yes Anything!,* emphasizes that guilt or remorse have no place in rational recovery, and one should simply refuse to feel these emotions.

RR literature comes across as being rather anti-AA. They particularly object to the belief in powerlessness over alcohol. I spoke to Dave Tripple, an RR advocate and director of a two-track chemical dependency program at Forest Health Systems, Inc. in Des Plaines, Illinois. His program is one of the few which gives clients a choice between AA and RR. Triple believes that people cannot be powerless over a liquid,[12] though he admits that after we take the first drink, we may well be powerless to resist the next drink (and the next, and the next) because alcohol affects our rational minds—which we need to retain our power over alcohol.

---

12. Dave Tripple, telephone interview, March 2, 1995.

Tripple also says that RR would consider it a waste of time to make amends with people from our pasts who no longer affect the course of our lives. A decision to make amends for the sake of making amends (or because one believes it is the *right* thing to do) would be a moral conviction. On the other hand it is rational to make amends with people with whom we still have contact. For example, you may have to patch up things with your family in order to be able to live in harmony with them, or you may need to assuage customers you hope to sell to in the future.

RR holds support group meetings like AA and SOS, but this organization is not nonprofit. Groups are generally run by a trained facilitator who is a professional therapist, and fees are charged. RR encourages total abstinence and requires that participants have a genuine desire to stop drinking.

QUAD A—Twenty years ago in Chicago, Don W. organized the first Quad A (Alcoholics Anonymous for Atheists and Agnostics) program. His group has continued to meet and Don W. and many other AA Twelve Steppers have remained sober these twenty years without the help of God.

Quad A meetings have sprung up in the greater Chicago area and in major cities across the country, quietly offering this AA alternative to those who see themselves as secularists, humanists, atheists, or agnostics. Though many areas offer AA meetings for agnostics, these do not necessarily reflect Quad A philosophy. Many AA agnostic meetings see themselves as a temporary way station or holding ground for new AA members who have not *yet* gotten God. The leaders of these groups still believe that one cannot get sober without a belief in God and presume that those who attend AA agnostic meetings will either get God and join mainstream AA or lose their sobriety because they refuse to give themselves over to God.

Not so Quad A. Atheism is considered a viable life stance.

Quad A has just begun to organize and publicize their existence so that more groups will be established. At the 1994 AA National Conference in San Diego, Quad A requested that a room be set aside for AA atheists and agnostics. They had no particular program but, rather, were just trying to get an idea about how many people would be interested in this alternative. The room was jammed with people throughout the entire weekend and Quad A developed a huge mailing list. The first Quad A newsletter was produced in April 1995, and they hope it will be a comfort to the many isolated atheist or agnostic AAs out there, as well as an inspiration to create many new Quad A groups.

Women for Sobriety—WFS is a sobriety organization that focuses on women's special concerns. Because she was put off by the male language and perspective in AA's Twelve Steps, Jean Kirkpatrick founded a new group for women. She had also found that men dominated the conversation at AA meetings, and recovering women had too much difficulty asserting themselves to gain equal time. She wanted to grant women the space to speak. Kirkpatrick feels that women have different reasons for drinking and therefore have different needs for a recovery program.

Kirkpatrick has written her own thirteeen Statements to replace the Twelve Steps. Her list concentrates on rebuilding self-esteem and self-empowerment in the women who attend WFS meetings. Kirkpatrick also believes in encouraging women to take care of their health during recovery by exercising, taking vitamins to replace the stores lost during alcoholic periods, and eating a healthy diet. She has a more holistic approach than AA.

In the appendix you will find the "Steps" or "Commitments" that are stated in many of the above alternative programs.

Forgiveness and Amends

Many of the alternative programs I have mentioned are critical of Twelve Step programs. They criticize the original Twelve Steps as fostering dependence and low self-worth. Why then have I chosen to keep this journal in a Twelve Step format?

Though Twelve Step programs may not be the answer for some, I believe that a restatement of the Twelve Steps can allow this program to be useful to a much wider range of people. For, despite its drawbacks, the Twelve Steps offer a sound philosophy and lifestyle that can benefit anyone.

The Twelve Steps focus on personal responsibility and strongly discourage blaming others for our troubles. They encourage the clearing away of bad feelings from the past so we can begin a new life free of resentments.

The Steps that encourage us to honestly assess our personal shortcomings support our ability to see our responsibility and agency in creating our own problems. Everyone, addicts and nonaddicts alike, has flaws. The exploration of these flaws need not send us into a self-recriminatory depression or lower our self-esteem. Good group support or support from a therapist should help us keep our shortcomings in perspective.

The Steps that encourage us to recall our wrongdoings and make amends also serve to teach us forgiveness and relieve guilt that may have been damaging to our self-esteem. We are encouraged to make amends even to those who have hurt us first or who have retaliated in hurtful ways, and we are expected to apologize even if our adversary does not admit his or her wrongs! Some see this as unhealthy self-debasement, but unilateral gestures are a keystone to good conflict resolution. Someone must begin the process of reconciliation.

If you have gone as far as you can to make amends and offer forgiveness, even though your opponent does not respond to you in kind, you have earned an end to guilt.

I believe that guilt and resentment undermine anyone's peace of mind and ability to enjoy life to the fullest. To be free and happy, you must do your part to end past conflicts. Then you truly can go forth to regard today as the first day of your new life.

Abstinence or Moderation?

Along with AA, SOS, and RR, I support total abstinence as the surest route to recovery. You can't get drunk if you don't take the first drink. Anyone who has attained a long period of sobriety after years of destructive drinking knows they have a great deal to lose if they try drinking again and fail to "control" it, and little to gain if they do manage to learn to drink moderately.

A new program called Moderation Management,[13] or MM,

13. "Moderation Management," *Newsweek,* (11 March, 1995).

aims to teach problem drinkers how to drink moderately. They claim that there are two kinds of problem drinkers: those who are physically addicted and those who are not. MM believes that the latter can learn to control their drinking through re-education. They recommend you begin with a three month period of abstinence after which you would try alcohol again and be trained to know your own limit. As the theory goes, you would be able to drink moderately thereafter.

Proposals of this type cause great dismay among Twelve Steppers and other abstinence advocates. Most alcoholics and users have quit for a period and tried to take up moderate use many times before, and they have learned that any substance use eventually leads to substance abuse. They think it is criminal to publicize these moderation schemes. Abstinence advocates usually publicly decry that these programs cannot work, even though they know that some can resume normal drinking.

There really are some people who can drink destructively for a period of time and then change to moderate drinking. Estimates given by opponents are that this works for less than 5 percent of destructive drinkers. I know quite a few people who have done it. Most of my college drinking buddies who abused alcohol and drugs with me for four steady years began to drink moderately (and completely quit using drugs) when they got their first responsible adult job or when they began to have children. For many college students destructive drinking is *circumstantial.*

An even more amazing case of circumstantial drinking is that of a woman named Henrietta whom I have known for over forty years. From the age of thirty-four to fifty-nine Henrietta drank destructively with her alcoholic husband. She would fall down, park her car on neighbors' lawns, and try to seduce her daughters' boyfriends while in alcoholic blackouts. When her husband died, Henrietta began dating a man who had heart problems and was under doctor's orders not to drink. Henrietta stopped getting drunk. She now has a beer on occasion. She is seventy-one years old and simply no longer drinks to drunkenness.

Because I think stories like this create a tremendous temptation that can undermine a person's tenuous commitment to abstinence, I wish I could insist this never happens. But if I deny that such people exist, and then you meet one, you would then have a right to doubt everything I have said.

So I tell you, yes, some people can return to moderate drinking. But don't try it yourself. You have little to gain, and too much to lose. *I'm* not about to try it.

Here's a quick self-test: If you have been worried enough to buy this book or read this far, you probably are not a candidate for MM.

Finding Your Group

Whether you believe in God, sincerely want to form a belief in a Greater Power, or are a confirmed secularist, this journal can help you begin your journey toward recovery and deliver you to the next step. While you are journal writing, I strongly recommend you find some supportive group to join. The easiest and most obvious choice is a Twelve Step program, and this option should not be an impossible alternative for non-Christians. If there is no SOS or RR group in your area and you are not comfortable starting one, then give a traditional Twelve Step group an honest try.

Seek out five different meetings in your area. Sometimes a companionable group of people who share most other interests with you can make your religious differences seem insignificant. The more groups you try, the more likely you are to find that special combination of people. Then choose the one you like the best and commit yourself to trying five meetings with this group. This will give you some foundation in the Twelve Step approach that you can take with you if you should decide to wing it on your own.

If you simply cannot get comfortable in a Twelve Step or other support group setting, in the workbook section I suggest other types of groups that you may find sufficiently supportive.

That Still Small Voice Within

On occasion the steps and the text will mention listening to your still small voice within, or your own better judgment. For many this advice may be premature.

Developing good judgment and knowing which of the internal voices you hear is that true, reliable still small voice often takes time and practice. Until you are able to follow your own judgment with confidence, it is good to use others as a sounding board. Your confidant could be a sponsor, a friend whose life you admire, or a therapist.

A therapist with knowledge about addictions can be invaluable for helping you make important decisions. They are committed to confidentiality as a profession and are trained to respond in a non-judgmental manner. They can be a tremendous source of support and a voice of reliable wisdom. With their help you can come to recognize your pure "still small voice within."

What This Book Is Not

Remember, this book is not a complete text to recovery. Its primary purpose is to offer stimulus to self-explorations that will build personal strength and help the journal writer set priorities as well as sort through options. In this introduction I have tried to touch upon all major problems associated with addiction and recovery and to refer the reader to sources that will provide more complete information. In addition, I have attempted to pull the best ideas from a diversity of programs to create a self-education tool.

Because I have tried to create a journal that would be useful to people suffering from a wide range of addictions and who represent a diversity of philosophical viewpoints, I could not possibly provide here all the information that all these people need. Therefore, throughout the journal I have recommended many informational texts as supplements. Though *which* texts you choose is an option based on personal needs and choice, reading supplemental texts, per se, should not be considered optional; it is required! You will need more information than I can provide here, and books are also an important source of *support* to those who feel alone with a problem.

Don't just read self-help materials. Check out medical, psychological, or other professional journals. Comb libraries, bookstore recovery sections, and sobriety support meetings and read, read, read.

Basic Texts

Outside AA, most organized Twelve Step groups have a basic text wherein they reword the Twelve Steps so that the text is more focused on that group's particular problem. For example, Overeaters Anonymous has its own Twelve Step book wherein the word *food* replaces the word *alcohol* where it would appear in the traditional Twelve Steps of AA. The explanations and stories in the overeaters' handbooks relate tales of eating binges rather than litanies of drunkenness. However, many of these Twelve Step organizations simply use the AA *Big Book* and ask attendees to "translate" the material as they read.

Though I will give brief explanations of each step, I cannot cover the nuances of every addiction in detail. You need to read the most relevant book you can find on your addiction. Following is an annotated bibliography that can help you select a good title, whether you are a theist or a maverick.

General

Arnold Washton and Donna Boundy, *Willpower's Not Enough*. New York: HarperPerennial, 1989.

This book is full of good practical advice and manages to give examples and address the problems of just about every addiction imaginable. The authors begin with explanations of how addictive patterns have been developed in our society, families, and self-concepts. This book is my overall favorite, and I recommend it to all readers.

Alcoholics

Alcoholics Anonymous, 3rd Edition. New York: Alcoholics Anonymous World Services, Inc., 1976. Write to: Alcoholics Anonymous, Box 459, Grand Central Station, New York, NY 10163, or call (212)870-3400.

This book is most commonly known as *The Big Book*. It was originally written by the founder of AA and explains its origins. The Twelve Steps are explained and many stories of others' recoveries are presented. However, the vast majority of the stories are about male drunks.

Twelve Steps and Twelve Traditions: An Interpretive Commentary on the A.A. Program. New York: Alcoholics Anonymous World Services, Inc., 1993. Write to: Alcoholics Anonymous, Box 459, Grand Central Station, New York, NY 10163, or call (212)870-3400.

This book is written for alcoholics. It explains each Step and tradition and adds insights offered by old timers as they recall working the steps themselves. The Twelve traditions happen to be a great framework for keeping any group focused and healthy.

Kerry M. Olitzky and Stuart A. Copans, *Twelve Jewish Steps to Recovery: A Personal Guide to Turning from Alcoholism and Other Addictions,* Woodstock, VT: Jewish Lights Publishing, 1991.

True to the Twelve Steps as originally written, this book presents accompanying text that uses stories and examples from the *Torah* and Jewish tradition.

Money Addictions

Debtor's Anonymous. Write to Debtors Anonymous, P.O. Box 400, Grand Central Station, New York, NY 10063-0400, or call (212)642-8220.

Sharing Recovery through Gamblers Anonymous. Los Angeles: Gamblers Anonymous, 1994. P.O. Box 17173, Los Angeles, CA 90010, or call (213)386-8789.

Drug Addictions

Narcotics Anonymous, 4th Edition. World Service Office, Inc., 1987. Write to: Narcotics Anonymous, P.O. Box 9999, Van Nuys, CA 91409, or call (818)780-3951.

Sex Addicts

Sex and Love Addicts Anonymous, Boston, MA: Augustine Fellowship, 1993.

This is the official publication of Sex and Love Addicts Anonymous, P.O. Box 88, New Town Branch, Boston, MA 92258.

Overeaters

The Twelve Steps of Overeaters Anonymous. Torrance, CA: Overeaters Anonymous, 1990. Write: Overeaters Anonymous, P.O. Box 92870, Los Angeles, CA 90009, or call (213)542-8363.

This book does an excellent job of translating the Twelve Steps into the language of food addiction.

Jack and Lois Trimpey, *Taming the Feast Beast.* New York: Delacorte Press, 1995. Check your local bookstore or write: Rational Recovery, c/o Lotus Press, Box 800, Lotus, CA 95651, or call (916)621-2667.

This is a non-theistic book on eating disorders and follows the basic method described in Jack Trimpey, *The Final Fix* (see page 24 for further information).

Codependents Anonymous

Melodie Beattie, *Codependent No More.* New York: Harper & Row, 1987.

This book began the codependency movement and is still the best of its kind. Beattie also wrote some follow-up books.

WORKAHOLICS

Diane Fassel, *Working Ourselves to Death: The High Cost of Workaholism and the Reward of Recovery.* San Francisco: HarperCollins, 1990.

Fassel recommends Workaholics Anonymous as the most effective way of dealing with compulsive working. To receive materials from Workaholics Anonymous write to Workaholics Anonymous, P.O. Box 289, Menlo Park, CA 94026, or call (510)273-9253.

FOR FAMILY MEMBERS

Al-Anon's Twelve Steps and Twelve Traditions. New York: AlAnon Family Group Headquarters, Inc., 1981. Write: Al-Anon Family Group Headquarters, Inc., P.O. Box 862, Midtown Station, New York, NY 10018-0862, or call (212)302-7240, or FAX (212)869-3757.

This book is written for family and friends of alcoholics. Co-dependents will also find the book helpful.

From Survival to Recovery: Growing Up in an Alcoholic Home. New York: Al-Anon Family Group Headquarters, Inc., 1994. Write: Al-Anon Family Group Headquarters, Inc., P.O. Box 862, Midtown Station, New York, NY 10018-0862, or call (212)302-7240, or FAX (212)869-3757.

This book is written for adult children of alcoholics and explains the Twelve Steps from their unique viewpoint.

Robert Custer, M.D. and Harry Milt, *When Luck Runs Out: Help for Compulsive Gamblers and Their Families.* New York: Facts on File Publications, 1985.

National Alliance for the Mentally Ill. Various Pamphlets. 200 N.

Glebe Rd., Suite 1015, Arlington, VA 22203-3754. Helpline: (800)950-NAMI

This is a support group for parents and caretakers of the chronically mentally ill who suffer from diseases such as schizophrenia and mood disorders. Mentally ill patients also find support there. Some have found Al-Anon groups helpful, too.

"Alternative" Readings for Secularists and Others

Living Sober, New York: Alcoholics Anonymous World Services, Inc., 1976. Write to: Alcoholics Anonymous, Box 459, Grand Central Station, New York, NY 10163, or call (212)870-3400.

Though an official AA publication, this book does not mention God. It assumes that you may be an agnostic or atheist and accepts this as a life-long religious stance for some people. It is packed with terrific advice for recovering alcoholics and will not make even the most dedicated atheist cringe. Because it does not mention any of the Twelve Steps, it may appeal to a great many alcoholics who are uncomfortable with the traditional Twelve Step approach.

James Christopher, *How to Stay Sober: Recovery without Religion*. Buffalo, NY: Prometheus Books, 1988. Available through bookstores or by contacting Prometheus Books, 59 John Glenn Drive, Buffalo, NY 14228-2197.

The first half of this book generally denounces AA methods, but the second half presents the SOS program for how to get sober and stay sober. The program is very practical and not totally incompatible with the Twelve Steps. If you are an atheist or agnostic, I highly recommend it. Christopher has also written *SOS Sobriety: The proven Alternative to Twelve-Step Programs* (1992) with the same publisher.

If you wish to join SOS or find out if there is a group near you, write: SOS National Clearinghouse, P.O. Box 5, Buffalo, NY 14215-0005, (716)834-2922.

Jean Kirkpatrick, *Turnabout: New Help for the Woman Alcoholic*. New York: Bantam, 1990.

Written by the founder of Women for Sobriety, this book presents the Thirteen Statements that Kirkpatrick feels are more appropriate for women. Write: Women for Sobriety, P.O. Box 618, Quakertown, PA 18951, or call (215)536-8026 or (800)333-1606.

Jack Trimpey, *The Final Fix for Alcohol and Drug Dependence: AVRT.* Lotus, CA: Rational Recovery, 1994. Write: Rational Recovery, c/o Lotus Press, Box 800, Lotus, CA 95651, or call (916)621-2667.

This book is rather critical of AA. Trimpey considers some of the Twelve Steps to be destructive. The main concept in the book, that the part of you that desires a drink is a "beast" and can be "killed," is a very useful metaphor for conquering a drinking problem.

If you decide you would like to join the Rational Recovery movement, write: Rational Recovery, P.O. Box 800, Lotus, CA 95651, or call (916)621-4374.

Martha Cleveland and Arlys G. Cleveland, *The Alternative Twelve Steps: A Secular Guide to Recovery.* Deerfield Beach, FL: Health Communications, 1992.

This book has masterfully kept the integrity of the Twelve Step program while restating the concepts with respect for secular views. It is a truly palatable "translation" and should serve as a gentle bridge between traditionalists and mavericks.

Jerry Dorsman, *How to Quit Drinking Without AA: A Complete Self-Help Guide.* Rocklin, CA: Prima Publishing, 1994. Check your local bookstore or write: Prima Publishing, PO Box 1260BK, Rocklin, CA 95677, or call (916)786-0426.

This book avoids putting down other programs and provides tons of information that AA literature overlooks. For example, Dorsman describes the toll on your health that alcoholism can take and recommends diet and exercise regimens that can help the body recover.

Charlotte Davis Kasl, Ph.D., *Many Roads, One Journey: Moving Beyond the Twelve Steps.* New York: HarperPerennial, 1992.

This book mainly presents a feminist perspective on the Twelve Steps and Twelve Step programs. It is critical of the prominence men play in "The Big Book" and other AA literature and objects to the assumption that the "Greater Power" is male (as shown in the language of the Twelve Steps.)

In addition to these basic texts, at the start of each chapter I recommend a book that might help you work that step. With one of the above resources in hand, you are ready to begin your journal program.

✦

How To Use The Twelve Step Journal

The *Twelve Step Journal* is designed to help you get the most out of your Twelve Step work through worksheets and journal writing and will reinforce the lessons you learn during your group work or reading. It may also serve as a companion if you live in an area without a Twelve Step group or other recovery group. Ideally, Twelve Stepping is an interactive process, and it is best to find a friend or group with whom to share explorations. (An understanding therapist can also be a good companion in your recovery.) The journal can help you structure your talks about the Twelve Steps.

I have focused on the four major groups who find Twelve Step work helpful or even essential to maintaining their sanity: alcoholics or drug addicts, co-dependents or ACOAs (adult children of alcoholics), workaholics, and overeaters. The members of each of these groups suffer from the results of either addictive or compulsive behavior. I hope their examples will be relevant to others in similar Twelve Step programs.

The Format

Each chapter covers one of the Twelve Steps and is laid out in the same general way. Part I describes the meaning of the step and helps you recognize feelings people have at this stage. Part II is the workbook section of the chapter. In it there is a series of tasks that help you gain insight into where you are in regard to that step. This is a short answer section that is meant to be a stimulus for your deeper journal reflections in Part III.

The first few exercises generally challenge you to make a realistic assessment of your life situation and why it must change. Because it is difficult to change when we are beaten down with self-recrimination, these exercises are followed by a "Breather" where you get to focus on the positive for a moment. The last few exercises help you to begin breaking down the problem or task into small manageable steps toward a solution or a brighter future. It is suggested that you do this work shortly after your first meeting or reading on that particular step.

However, keep in mind that these exercises are *not* a test! There are no wrong answers and the exercises may be approached in any way that allows you to feel comfortable doing them. People who are very newly sober may find that they still lack the ability to focus or concentrate and may initially be overwhelmed or confused by the exercises. This feeling will pass in time. Meanwhile, do what you can and move on. In a few weeks you can come back and try to complete more exercises.

Please remember that this is your private journal, and its purpose is to meet your individual needs. You are the one who knows best what your needs and capabilities are at this point. Tailor your work in the journal to suit yourself.

Relaxation

The ability to relax is such a bugaboo for the newly sober that it warrants special attention. For this reason, every step will have a portion of the exercises devoted to learning how to relax. Though there are many ways to relax, meditation is perhaps the most valuable. When one learns to meditate deeply, one begins to hear their still small voice within—that wise part of ourselves that always knows what is best for us, because no one else can know us as well as we can know ourselves. We are the only ones who have been there every moment of our lives, and so we have a wealth of information to draw from.

Because meditation is so valuable, I will devote many words to it here. However, when you come to the step exercises, I branch out and include very different means to relaxation (such as exercise or a warm bath). Meditation can be very difficult for the newly sober, and I want you to have many alternatives.

Kathi Bedard, MICA (Mental Illness/Chemical Abuse) specialist and therapist for the New Jersey Department of Human Services, is an expert teacher and practicer of meditation principles. With her permission, I recount here the advice she generally gives to her clients.

First of all, keep in mind that everyone is different. We do not all respond equally well to the same stimulus. For example, 10 percent of the population finds it impossible to do visualization exercises. They are likely to respond better to auditory stimuli such as recordings of the ocean.

Second, we must remind ourselves that meditation is meant to be a letting go. Many initially have difficulty meditating because they are worrying about doing it "correctly." If bothersome thoughts keep intruding when you have been told that you should empty your mind, your frustration will be compounded by the fact that you now feel you are "failing" at meditating. Try to avoid this kind of self-judging. Those of you who are very anxious may find it easier to do more active relaxing (such as vigorous exercising).

For the willing and able, Kathi Bedard offers this series of progressive meditation techniques:

1. **The beginning**

   Sit in a comfortable position, preferably with your feet flat and in contact with the ground. This will help you to maintain minimal contact with your surroundings, called "grounding." This lessens the anxiety from the unknown that you may feel about the experience. Don't lie down. Meditating is different from sleeping.

   Place one hand on your abdomen with your thumb resting at your navel, and one hand on your chest. Practice breathing so that only the hand on your abdomen moves. Breathing is vital to life. If you are breathing into your abdomen, you will be unable to feel anxiety. If you were able to focus on your breathing and think of nothing else, you have begun to meditate. But don't worry if you have intruding thoughts, even the great gurus have such thoughts from time to time. However, they don't worry about it. They just gently bless these thoughts and go on.

2. **The Next Step**

Sit in a comfortable position with feet flat on the ground. Close your eyes, place your palms flat on your legs. Begin abdominal breathing. Breathe in through your nose for a slow count of 8, hold your breath for a count of 4, breathe out through your mouth for a count of 8. Continue this exercise for as long as you like. You may want to do this meditation to some soft tonal music or to the aroma of oils or incense.

Focus on the spot just below your navel, where your hand rested as you were learning to breathe. Just pay attention to that area. This is called "centering yourself." If you notice that you feel a loss of sensation in your physical body, let it happen. This is the gift you get for concentrating on your inner self.

3. **More advanced**

Begin abdominal breathing as above; center yourself. As you breathe in, picture a golden thread that runs in through your nose, reaching down into that spot just below your navel. As you exhale, picture the thread running up your back and out from your mouth, creating a golden light that wraps around you. When the thread reaches the spot just below your navel, picture a glowing mass of energy that mingles with the thread and circulates throughout your body. Think "inhale one, exhale one" as you breathe (or some similar thought such as "I breathe in, I breathe out," or "I am relaxing, I am worthy," etc.). If your meditation has deepened, you may feel like you are floating, sinking, or physically numb. This is a good thing. As tension is released your muscles may twitch or jump. This is the natural process of letting go of fear and anxiety. If you are within the 10 percent who can't visualize, you may want to concentrate more on physical sensations, such as the coolness when you inhale and the heat of the exhale.

4. **Even more advanced**

Abdominal breathing, center . . .

As you breathe, using the steps above, picture a little tornado that spins off from the golden thread. This tornado absorbs discomfort and anxiety. On an exhale, send the tornado to collect tension or discomfort that you feel, beginning at your head, working your way down. As you breathe in, collect the tension, pull it into the pathway of the golden thread, and exhale it out through your mouth. Breathing in, create another tornado, exhale, and send it to work. Breathe in, collect, and exhale the tension. Repeat until the whole body is cleansed. If you experience a particularly strong sensation, breathe extra deeply, and exhale with force after you collect the sensation.

After the little tornado has done its job, just let your mind rest. Acknowledge any thoughts that wander in without judgment. This exercise can be done anywhere, any time you find yourself feeling tense.

The more you practice these techniques, the easier the process will become. When being centered becomes easy, your body will develop a built-in signal that tells you it has happened. Think of your meditation time as a mini-vacation for the soul, or a time to talk with an old dear friend (that still small voice.)

The Search for Meaning

Many of us have grown up in a religious tradition chosen by our families and may have experienced great disillusionment because of the difficulties we've experienced in life. For example, since alcoholism is hereditary, most addicts were raised by addicted parents. Though the parents may have avoided church for themselves, they still might have dropped the kids off at Sunday school. Chances are there was a great disparity between the values the church taught and the way the parents' lived their lives. As children we may have been told that if we are good, and we pray, God will grant our wishes. But God never stopped our parents from drinking or fighting no matter how good we were or how nicely we asked.

Hence, we may have come to adulthood with very strong feelings about what we don't believe (in a benevolent white-bearded man in the sky that grants wishes), but little understanding of what we do believe.

Yet, we all have beliefs and values that affect our lives, whether we are conscious of them or not. If we do not bring these beliefs to consciousness, they may undermine our sobriety.

In the journal sections titled "The Search for Meaning,"[1] there will be exercises and activities that will help us sort out what our beliefs and values are now, and whether or not we want to challenge them.

Directions for Part III: On-Going Step Work

Part III presents on-going, deeper Step work. These sections are consistent throughout the chapters and are meant to be an opportunity for you to freely explore the meaning of each step and the ways in which you will carry them out. Through open-ended writing, you can let insights emerge as you are ready to deal with them. This is how the psyche heals itself. Part III gives you the space and flexibility you need to become a partner with your psyche.

Twelve Step groups take many different formats depending on the area in which they are held. In large cities one can sometimes find a group that explores one step on an on-going basis. People move from one group to the next as they feel ready to tackle the next step.

In smaller towns there are usually not enough groups to allow this approach. Some groups may cycle through the steps regularly to provide meetings relevant to the broad and varied population they serve. Those working Step 1 listen in as those who are working Step 8 begin to talk about the process of making amends. Still other groups try to "go with the flow" and spend as many weeks on a particular step as the group seems to need and then selects the next step to move to by popular demand.

Some groups are a collection of people who have been meeting

1. Many of these exercises are derived from suggestions in the book *On the Path: Spirituality for Youth and Adults*, Boston: Beacon Press, 1989.

together for over ten years; other groups can change totally from week to week with the moderator as the only consistent person in the group. Part III is designed to serve the needs of the journal writer in all these situations.

Not only may we have little control over the order in which we address the steps in our meetings, we may have little control over the order in which we address the steps in our minds. We may find ourselves so preoccupied with someone to whom we owe amends that we cannot concentrate on developing our personal stance on, or understanding of, a "higher power." The journal can help relieve this pressure. You can flip ahead to Chapter 8 and write about the wrong you have done your friend and what you plan to do about it.

This serves three purposes: 1) it provides an opportunity to get the guilt off our chests, 2) it assures that we will not forget to make amends to this person later, and 3) as any experienced Twelve Stepper knows, we can make a real mess of things if we actually try to skip over Steps 4, 5, 6, and 7 and rush out to make amends. When we have finished these earlier steps and are finally ready to make amends, the journal exercises in Step 8 will help us think through our actions and their possible consequences so we can handle the situation better.

Therefore you should feel free to jump around in the sections of Part III, not only within the particular chapter you are focusing on, but also hopping ahead to other chapters when a relevant thought or insight needs to be recorded before it is lost. Remember, Twelve Step work is not always linear. Many find that they work through certain steps (particularly Steps 4 through 7) several times before they are ready to move on. Because we can never anticipate which section will mean the most to any individual, a number of blank pages have been provided at the end of the book to continue important entries that do not fit in the space provided.

How to Respond to the Sections in Part III

In each chapter, we will repeat the same sequence of sections. The following is an explanation of the type of material one might explore in each of them:

NOTE: MARK THIS PLACE FOR EASY REFERENCE

You will need to refer to these explanations as you come to the heading under each step.

1. Stories of others that have helped me see myself.

Storytelling is a great part of Twelve Step work. If our minds are open, we can learn a great deal from the experiences of others. Indeed, it is sometimes easier to look at ourselves when we hear the foibles of others. We can do this privately before we are ready to share our own stories. This section is provided so that you can write the stories that have produced an "aha!" experience for you. It is also wise to record stories that particularly move you even if you don't understand why at the time. The meaning of these stories may become clearer to you later.

2. Relevant dreams.[2]

Our dreams are direct messages from our unconscious. They can often tell us what we are thinking, feeling, or fearing long before these insights become known to our conscious minds. They are like a preview of insights to come. Some people have done a lot of dream work and can quickly recognize and characterize the important messages their dreams are sending them. But remember, dreams are not memories, though we may sometimes dream about something we remember. Dreams are mainly symbolic and should be interpreted as such.

If you are new to dream work, you may just want to begin recording the dreams that you can capture, especially those accompanied by strong feelings. By looking back at these dreams months later, you may begin to learn how to interpret your dreams and what they tell you about your readiness for and reactions to your Twelve Step work.

It is generally believed that everyone dreams, though about 10 percent of the population seem to be incapable of remembering their dreams. Before you decide you are part of that 10 percent, follow these suggestions.

Though dreams are often forgotten by morning, many people

awake in the night at the end of a dream. Keep a pen and pad at your bedside and begin writing down your dreams as soon as you awaken. (For those who hate to write, a tape recorder all set to go will serve as well.) I have even found it possible to write in the dark without seeing what I'm writing, so don't use the excuse that you will disturb your roommate.

As you begin paying careful attention to capturing dreams, you will discover your own dream rhythm. For example, you may find that if you set your alarm to go off at 6 A.M. (instead of your usual 7 A.M. awakening), you are caught in the middle of a dream. Have your pen and pad ready. Dreams must be written down, or told to someone, or you will probably totally forget them within an hour.

Some people can even do "lucid dreaming." They can decide before going to sleep what they would like to dream about and instruct themselves to do so. You can also instruct yourself to remember a dream, and your mind will often obey you.

3. *Confessions.*

Sometimes we see things we don't like about ourselves long before we are ready to open our mouths and tell another person. Because our memories tend to filter out the unpleasant and record the things that make us think better of ourselves, it is sometimes wise to keep an on-going account of our offenses. When we are trying to make a fearless inventory of ourselves, all our faults may be distant memories. By checking back in our confessions section we can retain some humility. As they say, confession is good for the soul. It does help to admit what we have done, even if only to ourselves. It is the first step toward self-forgiveness.

4. *Small Achievements and Stepping Stones.*

As we begin our Twelve Step journey in earnest, we will find ourselves taking many small steps toward change. One by one they seem insignificant, but as they accumulate they are what make up the fabric of deep change. Something as simple as apologizing for being late rather than defensively giving all the reasons why (traffic, last minute phone call, etc.), particularly if this is a new behavior, is a significant sign of change that should be recorded. If you are co-dependent, whenever you resist the temptation to do someone else's work, you should record it. If you are a workaholic at your job or as a volunteer, be sure to note every time you hear yourself say, "No."

By keeping track of all these small steps you will consciously build your new history of living in healthier ways. You will find rereading these sections reassuring when you are feeling stuck.

Psychology has long recognized that we grow in spurts. Each of these spurts is usually accompanied by a significant insight or experience that creates some kind of turning point. We do not change all at once, but in steps. Frequently we take a step backward, and it is easier to find our way forward again if we can remember the step we took to get there. For example, maybe you have always wanted to be less shy—to be able to just walk up and talk to people at parties, sober. But what you have normally done in the past is avoid parties altogether, or get smashed before you go so you lose your inhibitions.

Perhaps your first step—the one that becomes the first stepping stone to eventually conquering shyness—is to sign up for an adult interest course. This may be less threatening than walking into a party cold because you can talk about the task at hand instead of having to grope for topics of conversation. The more experiences you build up where you have not used substances to relax to talk to people, the easier it will be to face new situations.

But stepping stones are not necessarily planned moves. They are often recognized retrospectively. By looking back and discovering how changes began, we can better understand how to create change in ourselves. This is why we record our stepping stones. In each chapter you record the stepping stones that helped you achieve the goals of that step. This is something you may do immediately or months after leaving a step, or you may realize you have already undergone a change that has started you on the road to completing a future step.

5. Conflicts and their resolution or nonresolution.

Even more pointedly than dreams, conflicts clarify what we need to change and how we are feeling about what is happening in our lives right now. Most people hate conflicts and would not only like to avoid them, they would also like to avoid thinking about them. But conflicts are our greatest teachers. Every time you have an argument with someone (or an internal conflict over a decision you have to make), describe it in your journal. Soon you will see a pattern and be able to recognize what "pushes your buttons" or what you do to push the buttons of others. Resolution of conflict begins with recognition. As you work your way through the journal, you will see exercises and advice on how to better deal with conflict.[3]

6. Reflections.

This is your most open-ended section. Be sure to date each entry, for this will be a log of your progress across time. This is for all the thoughts that step work sparks that don't fit into any other category. You might write in it daily or weekly. Regular journal writing will not only help you explore insights, it will also allow you to expel tension or fears.

You can hop around through different chapters writing reflections or insights related to particular steps as they come to you, or you can use this section as a diary by making your first entries in the Reflections section of the first chapter, then continuing in chronological order through the Reflections sections of the following chapters. However you decide to approach it, think of this as your "free space."

✦

3. Many of the conflict resolution exercises are derived from the curriculum for the Alternatives to Violence course offered by Peace Grows. To contact Peace Grows write to them at Humanity House, 513 West Exchange St., Akron, OH, 44307 or call (216)864-5442.

THE STEPS

✦

STEP 1

We admitted we were powerless over our addiction/compulsion—that our lives had become unmanageable.[1]

Part I: The Meaning of Step 1[2]

The central task of Step 1 is to recognize that our lives are beyond our control, and we cannot continue our superhuman efforts at patching up the many mistakes we make. We recognize that it is time to move from a *crisis mode* to a *prevention mode.*

Here are some familiar patterns:

Alcoholics or drug abusers find that no one will believe their promises to change anymore.

Overeaters recognize that all diets have ultimately failed and that they are now facing life-threatening illness.

Co-dependents find they are too ill or exhausted to go on doing everyone's work and that others have become more and more resistant to the co-dependent's efforts to control them.

---

1. Some of the Twelve Steps have been altered to accommodate a greater diversity of outlooks. AA's original Twelve Steps appear in the appendix.

2. Begin the basic text of your choice or read Arnold Washton and Donna Boundy, *Willpower's Not Enough* (New York: HarperPerennial, 1989). Secularists may wish to read Martha Cleveland and Arlys G, *The Alternative Twelve Steps: A Secular Guide to Recovery* (Deerfield Beach, FL: Health Communications, 1992).

Workaholics find deadlines passing by unmet, forget to write down appointments, or fall ill with no "contingency plan."

ACOAs become so overwhelmed by their standards and commitments that they cannot get out of bed to act on anything.

Some peoples' lives had become unmanageable *before* they became addicted, and they began using their addiction to try to escape their painful lives.

People often have trouble recognizing their on-going patterns. In Step 1 we realize that our addictions are not temporary situations created by our bosses, our lovers, our children, our health, the time of year, or the weather. It is often helpful to review all the attempts we have made to correct the problem and see how they have ultimately failed.

We may have ignored the physical, emotional, and spiritual reasons why our addiction has held us hostage. In alcohol, drug, and food addictions, there is often a physical craving that defeats our best resolve. As co-dependents we may receive a "rush" as we imagine ourselves saving our loved ones. This creates a surge in adrenaline and other body chemicals that we will probably crave again.

Our addiction also becomes a distraction that protects us from feeling our loneliness, experiencing feelings of inadequacy, or remembering painful past events that we cannot change. Our sense of spiritual emptiness may create despair—the feeling that we have never had enough, and we will *never* have enough because we are selfish and insatiable.

We have taken an important step when we are ready to admit aloud that our lives have become unmanageable. Dysfunctional behavior thrives in silence. As part of this step we admit our failures to others. After writing in your journal and clarifying your thoughts on this step, you will need to select one or two people to tell. Safe choices are usually a therapist and someone from a support group that understands your problem.

Chances are that the people you feel close to are also the people you have hurt. You may be anxious to confess or apologize, but this can be very risky.

"Breaking the ice" about your new recognition of your addiction and your sincere desire to change is as far as you should go at this point. Don't give in to your desire to rush ahead to Step 9 and get everything off your chest. Making amends in a satisfying way that will yield good results for you takes careful planning. The steps are in a particular order for a good reason. Steps 4, 5, 6, 7, and 8 will teach you what you need to know to apologize and make amends (Step 9) effectively. If you feel great pressure to apologize, flip ahead to Step 8 in your journal and write out your confession. It will be safe there, waiting for you until you are ready to deal with it.

Don't expect applause when you admit that your life has become unmanageable because of your own behavior. Your listener may first feel relief and the buoyant hope that you will change, but once this euphoria passes those you have hurt may feel you are ripe to hear their complaints. They may confront you with every wrong you have committed for the past several years. This can be overwhelming, and you may begin to feel very defensive.

Don't be paralyzed by the guilt, remorse, or shame that these accusations spark. You need not accept the blame for every family problem. A general apology from you may dissipate some of the anger being aimed at you and give you a sense of having taken a step toward reparation. Say that you are sorry for your part in the problems and that you will be working to sort out why and how you've hurt others in the past. Ask for their patience. Remember that it's unrealistic to expect old resentments and hurts to just vanish now that you are sober, so you will need to have patience with them, too.

In Step 1 we learn to let down our armor and admit to ourselves that others can be trusted, even "providence" itself can be trusted. We strive to stop blaming others for our lapses. We come to understand that others rarely act out of malice. We are hurt not by their actions, but rather by the way *our expectations do not match up with reality.*

The solution is for us to change our expectations. That is the only element we can control.

When all our past efforts have failed, we need to take three deep breaths and allow new solutions, radical new ideas—uncensored—to drift into our minds and start us off in a fresh new direction.

The exercises in the workbook section of this chapter are designed to help the journal writer recognize the seriousness and pervasiveness of his or her addiction. The last few workbook exercises begin to point the journal writer in a new direction by helping him or her break down the tasks that make up a solution.

Remember, this is not a test. There are no wrong answers. This is for your eyes and your benefit. If you draw a blank on one of these exercises, skip it and move on.

✦

Part II: Workbook Section on Step 1

Task A—Evidence

I know my life has become unmanageable and unpredictable because some of the following things have been happening: (Check all that apply)

_____ Missed appointments
_____ Blank spells, memory lapses ("I totally forgot!")
_____ Unable to remember how or when I got home
_____ Canceling exercise or relaxation time to respond to over-commitments
_____ Putting loved ones on the back burner
_____ Headaches, illness
_____ Excessive expenditures
_____ Social withdrawal and isolation
_____ Short-temperedness
_____ Embarrassing or humiliating incidents
_____ Other (describe)____

____

____

✦

Task B—My Victims

List the people you have let down recently and describe how in one line.

1. ______________________ How? ______________________

____

2. ______________________ How? ______________________

____

3. ______________________ How? ______________________

____

Are there others who have told you that you let them down? Report here what they said.

____

____

____

✦

Task C—Painful Incidents

List and briefly describe three painful embarrassments, disappointments or conflicts that have happened in the recent past due to the unmanageability of your life:

1. ____

____

____

____

2. ____

____

____

____

3. ____

____

____

____

✦

BREATHER!

Task D—Pats On The Back

List and describe three things you managed to do well this month:

1. ____
____
____
____

2. ____
____
____
____

3. ____
____
____
____

How were you able to make these things happen? How can you make more good things happen in the future?

____
____
____

✦

Task E—New Patterns

Take one of your recent failings described in B or C and explain how you could have handled the situation differently. What steps could you take to avoid something like this happening again in the future? Make one small commitment to action.

Incident: ____

____

How I could have handled it differently:

____

____

____

____

____

____

Commitment: ____

____

____

____

✦

Task F—Failed Attempts

What attempts have I made in the past to control my addiction that have ended in failure?

Attempts:

____

____

____

What did I allow to defeat me? Is there a common thread?

____

____

____

✦

Task G—Before Unmanageability

Can you remember a time when your life seemed peaceful and uncomplicated? Describe this time and then try to remember when things took a decided turn for the worst. What incident or insight forced you to see that your life had become unmanageable? Record it here for future reference.

How I was: ____

____

____

____

____

____

Turning Point: ___

___

___

What would it take to turn your life back around?

___

___

Or do you believe your life has never been "manageable?" Why? Which of these factors can be changed?

___

___

___

✦

Task H—Reaching Out

Whom will you select to tell about your newfound insights? Who can listen to you tell about how your life has become unmanageable without saying "I told you so" or using the knowledge against you?

In the first column list the names of five people you might tell. (Consider anyone who is "a phone call away.") Then in the second column note **S** for safe, **R** for risky, and **B** for bad choice. When this is done, rank order them in the third column, and plan to speak to the most receptive person as soon as possible. Remember, a therapist might be one good choice.

___ ___ ___

___ ___ ___

___ ___ ___

___ ___ ___

___ ___ ___

✦

Task I—Relaxation Suggestion

Go to your public library and browse their audio tape listings (under subject "relaxation"). Check out three to five different tapes to try. Many offer muscle relaxation exercises, guided meditations, or soothing music with instruction. Two good tapes I found at my library were *Relax, Renew and Renenergize* by Adele Greenfield (Career Track Publications, 1988) and *Letting Go of Stress* by Emmett E. Miller, M.D. (Source Cassette Learning Systems, 1985).

Bring these home and try them out during the next week or so until you find a favorite that works well for you. You might want to ask your local record shop or bookstore to order you a copy for future use. Repetitition of the same tape often increases your ability to relax with the tape, cutting down the time each session that it takes for you to fall into a deeply relaxed state. After awhile you may not even be aware of hearing the tape, but it will continue to relax and mesmerize you.

✦

THE SEARCH FOR MEANING

Task J—Religious Viewpoints

World-wide there are many other religions or systems of belief. The immigration of people from diverse cultures to the United States has brought many new concepts and a diversity of beliefs that can enrich us. Below are some thumbnail sketches of just a few of the different religious positions or beliefs. I hope this expands your horizons as you try to discover or formulate your own beliefs.

Agnostic: Believes there is not enough evidence to prove or disprove the existence of God. Some are actively searching for a set of beliefs; others have no desire to think about the subject.

Atheist: Does not believe in the existence of God or any supreme being. However, they are not amoral. Many have healthy values and believe in leaving the world a better place than they found it. They do what they believe is right even without a "god" watching over them.

Buddhist: A follower of the teachings of Buddha, a wise prophet who taught that anyone can find enlightenment and end their cycle of reincarnation.

Calvinism: A Christian sect that assumes that all people are born sinners and only a few would be saved. Calvin taught *predestination* or the belief that the course of our lives has been decided before birth.

Christian: One who believes that Jesus is the son of God, sent to suffer for our sins. Most believe in an afterlife where one is sent to heaven or hell. Their holy book is the *Bible*.

Communitarian: One who believes that we are all interconnected and must consider the impact of our actions on our community, be it neighborhood, town, country, or planet.

Feminist Theology: Concerns itself with the "female" influence in religion. They commonly study ancient cultures where goddesses were worshipped rather than a male deity.

Humanist: Believes that humankind is the pinnacle of creation and has deep concerns about human welfare, values, and dignity.

Judaism: Belief in God as the unitary moral guiding force. One can understand God through interpretation of the Old Testament. One's life on earth is more important than afterlife concerns.

Paganism: Once used pejoratively as a synonym for hedonism, it is more recently associated with Wicca or the revival of nature-based religious practices that preceded Christianity.

Pantheist: God is a quality found in all things in the universe. Plants, animals, and humans all have some "god" in them.

Polytheism: A belief in many gods or goddesses that have individual powers as in the myths of ancient Greeks or Romans.

Unitarian-Universalism: Combines the Universalist belief that we are all born good with the belief that all the world's religions are valid. Each individual should form a personal theology.

These are just a few of the many choices available to you. Here are a few more terms that you may care to research:
Amish, Christian Science, Congregationalism, Deism, Existentialism, Evangelism, Hinduism, Islam, Mysticism, Metaphysics, Nihilism, Optimism, Pentecostal, Pessimism, Realism, Reincarnation, Rosicrucianism, Secularism, Situational Theology, Skepticism, Spiritualism, Transcendentalism, and Quaker (Society of Friends).

You may still prefer not to join any religious sect, but learning about them may clarify your own personal beliefs and values.

✦

Task K—Childhood Religion

What was the religion your family practiced or claimed?

____

How would you evaluate that religion?

Positive Aspects	**Negative Aspects**
____________________	____________________
____________________	____________________
____________________	____________________
____________________	____________________
____________________	____________________

When, how, and why did you break with that religion or why have you stayed with that religion?

____

____

____

Suggestion: You might want to ask your former or current clergy person if he or she knows other recovering people with whom you can get together.

✦

Part III: On-Going Step Work

For the categories listed below, please refer to the explanations given in the introduction. (See page 34) Remember, you may choose to skip around from step to step in these sections. Let your insights lead the way.

✦ 1. Stories of others that have helped me see myself (my addiction, the unmanageability of my life, etc.)

✦ 1. Stories of others that have helped me see myself *(Continued)*

✦ 2. Relevant dreams.

✦ 2. Relevant dreams. *(Continued)*

✦ 3. Confessions.

(Here is a place to write about some of the regrets and remorse you have begun to feel. Get it out of your system here rather than approaching directly the people you have hurt. This is a delicate matter that takes much careful planning and greater insight than you yet have.)

✦ 3. Confessions. *(Continued)*

✦ 4. Small Achievements and Stepping Stones.
(Brief descriptions.)

✦ 5. Conflicts and their resolution or nonresolution.

✦ 5. Conflicts and their resolution or nonresolution. *(Continued)*

✦ 5. Conflicts and their resolution or nonresolution. *(Continued)*

✦ 6. Reflections. (Date each entry)

✦ 6. **Reflections.** (Date each entry) *(Continued)*

✦ 6. Reflections. (Date each entry) *(Continued)*

✦ 6. Reflections. (Date each entry) *(Continued)*

✦ 6. Reflections. (Date each entry) *(Continued)*

STEP 2

We came to believe that, like all human beings, our power was limited and we needed to learn to let go and learn from others.

Part I: The Meaning of Step 2[1]

First we need to realize how insane our lives had become under the influence of our addiction. The overeater displays irrational and self-destruction eating patterns, eating to the point of extreme physical discomfort despite unhappiness with his weight and despite any and all health warnings. The alcoholic drinks and drives, endangering her life and everyone else's on the road. The drug addict lies, steals, borrows, or gets cash on credit cards until he is thousands of dollars in debt. These are not the acts of rational human beings.

The ACOA or other co-dependent needs to realize that he never had, and never will have, control over someone else's life, actions, or drinking. Not only can't he cure it, he didn't *cause* it. If he continues to try and save his loved one from her addiction, he will continue to feel worthless and useless. But if the co-dependent can let go and let the natural consequences of the addict's behavior come down on her, the addict will be that much closer to hitting bottom.

For both addicts and would-be rescuers, their entire systems of thinking become distorted. We surround ourselves with "birds of our feathers" so our lifestyles can continue unchallenged. We scoff at

1. You may wish to read Melvyn Kinder, *Mastering Your Moods* (Simon & Schuster, 1994).

others who are not "in the know." We feel we are sane as long as we act like others in our crowd.

All the while we are creating a polarized existence between the "good guys" like us and the "uncool." Everything in life becomes divided along rigid lines denoting "good" or "bad." Most tragically, we often reverse the traditional meaning of good and bad, assigning the white hats to our fellow addicts. These distorted perceptions keep us locked in unhealthy thinking patterns. In order to get well we will need to learn to see shades of gray.

People who are stoned or drunk are often forgetful, selfcentered, self-serving, irresponsible, and disloyal as soon as another's needs interferes with theirs. When fellow addicts are our most common companions, we begin to distort. We believe everyone is as self-centered as the addict, therefore we believe the whole of humanity is cold and uncaring. After all, if this is how our "friends" treat us, what can we expect from our enemies?

At the end of years of addiction, we have little trust in anyone and little hope for the human race. Driven by compulsion rather than reason, we have often done things of which we are ashamed. Many of us thought of suicide and some attempted it. We often have no altruistic feelings left, so we find it difficult to believe that anyone else has true altruistic feelings. We cannot trust ourselves, and we cannot trust others.

How do we get out of this black hole? We need to develop some faith—faith that there is at least one human being we can trust, faith that there is a program that can help us with our addiction if we faithfully follow it to its conclusion. We need to forbid ourselves to murmur "yes, but" when suggestions are offered to us. We must stop saying "no" to things before we have even tried them.

Often our judgment has become very poor because we have clouded our brain with irrational thinking for so long. Only irrational thinking would allow us to carry on with our addiction. Now we need to borrow from or "trust" someone else's judgment until our own has been restored to a healthy state.

Open the door to confide in someone you can count on. Look up an old friend who dropped out of your crowd or dropped you when the addiction got out of hand. Choose someone who is *happy* without alcohol, drugs, or compulsive behaviors.

Or make new friends. Be careful where you seek them out. Attend Twelve Step meetings and attach yourself to someone with several years of sobriety who is comfortable with him or herself. Join a group with an altruistic goal. Seek out a church or synagogue or other place of worship if you are not turned off by the thought of God or totally opposed to organized religion. (Or join the Unitarian-Universalist Church. Believe it or not, they welcome atheists and have no creed or doctrine.) Try the Sierra Club or Amnesty International. Campaign for a politician you really believe in. Surround yourself with people who think of others and are trying to leave the world a better place than they have found it.

Then brace yourself. For true faith only comes after you have weathered a disappointment. Your new friend may be out of town or sick with the flu when you need him most. Then you will practice patience, forgiveness, and the postponement of gratification. These are skills you need to get by in the real world, not a world full of deceit and dishonesty, but a world of fallible, limited (though often well-meaning) people. Life is frustrating and if we cannot tolerate frustration, we'll never make it.

True relationships teach us that we can trust others, that we are lovable and that sometimes we must take care of ourselves. As we gain friends who can help us get through and even enjoy most days, we feel ready to trust ourselves again.

As you keep faith with this process you will discover the joys of finding common ground, unconditional love, and a magical sense of connectedness that will leave you as high as any drug, drink, or new dress.

✦

Part II: Workbook Section on Step 2

(Work the tasks below at your own pace.)

Task A—Irrationality

Describe three irrational, insane, or embarrassing series of events that happened since your addiction took control.

1. (incident)____

How did you rationalize this to yourself later? Whom or what did you blame?

2. (incident) ____

How did you rationalize this to yourself later? Whom or what did you blame?

3. (incident) ____

____

____

____

How did you rationalize this to yourself later? Whom or what did you blame?

____

____

✦

Task B—Potential Friends

List Ten people at work, in your neighborhood, in your family, or in your acquaintanceship that you have avoided because they did not use your substance of choice (cocaine, alcohol, food, self-sacrifice, etc.) or did not overindulge as you did.

1. ______________	6. ______________
2. ______________	7. ______________
3. ______________	8. ______________
4. ______________	9. ______________
5. ______________	10.______________

In Column 1 name three of the above people you will try to get to know this month and in Column 2 indicate whether you plan to make your first contact by phone, at the water cooler, by the fence, or whatever other specific action is liable to bring you in contact with the person. In Column 3 write down the date by which you pledge to make the first contact. Then sign the pledge below the columns.

	Name	Method	Date
1.	______________________	________________________	_____
2.	______________________	________________________	_____
3.	______________________	________________________	_____

PLEDGE: I pledge to initiate three social contacts each with the above people this month. I will withhold all judgment or assessment of each person until I have seen them two more times.

____

SIGNATURE

✦

BREATHER!

Task C—Old Friends

Recall three of the best friends you had in your childhood, adolescence, and young adulthood. Describe them. Then decide what you liked best about them and speculate on what they liked best about you.

1. Childhood friend: ________________________________

Description: ________________________________

His or her best quality: ________________________________

Your best quality: ________________________________

2. Adolescent friend: ________________________________

Description: ________________________________

____

His or her best quality: ________________________________

Your best quality: ________________________________

3. Young adulthood friend: ________________________________

Description: ________________________________

____

His or her best quality: ____________________

Your best quality: ____________________

✦

Task D—Trustworthy Friends

Select three people you are either in touch with now, or would like to hunt up from your past, that you feel are trustworthy. Contact each by mail or phone. Select any of the three you feel are safe bets and plan a visit with him or her.

1. Name ____________________

address ____________________

Phone ____________________ Contact date ____________

Future plan ____________________

2. Name ____________________

Address ____________________

Phone ____________________ Contact date ____________

Future plan ____________________

3. Name ____________________

Address ____________________

Phone ____________________ Contact date ____________

Future Plan ____________________

✦

Task E—New Groups

1. Check any and all of the following whose values you believe you could share.

______ Twelve Step group
______ SOS (Secular Organization for Sobriety)
______ RR (Rational Recovery)
______ Conservative Christian church
______ Liberal Christian church
______ New Age church
______ Unitarian Universalist or non-Christian church
______ Synagogue
______ Non-religious ethical organization such as American Humanists' Association
______ Health club or team sport
______ Sierra Club or other environmental group
______ Amnesty International or other activist group
______ Scouts, Campfire or other work with youth
______ Computer Club
______ Writers' Group
______ Photography Club
______ Art Association or Museum
______ Adult Education class
______ Other ____

2. Rank order your selections by placing the number 1 before your first choice on the list, 2 by your second choice and so on.

3. Find out when and where your top three groups meet.

Club or group	**Location**	**Meeting time**
______________	______________	______________
______________	______________	______________
______________	______________	______________

4. Begin your social skill building by planning to attend one of each of these meetings. Try to arrive early and introduce yourself to whomever is standing around. Ask them if they are new and why they have come to the meeting or what they have enjoyed about the meetings. Tell him or her you are exploring

new interests and hoping to make new friends. When you are seated, smile and say hello to the people on either side of you. After the meeting, do not flee the room immediately. Stand around and try to strike up a conversation about the content of the meeting.

5. After you have explored your three interests commit to attending at least three more meetings of your favorite.

My favorite group:____

Names of person(s) I met: ________________________________

Next meeting date: ____________Time ____________Place __________

Write this information on your appointment calendar. Write in the following two meetings if you know the dates.

✦

Task F—Anticipation

What are you looking forward to most—

This week? ____

This month? ____

This year? ____

✦

Task G—Relaxation Suggestion

Play can be incredibly rejuvenating. Often we have lost the ability to "waste time" without guilt, but relaxation through structured play can be a great bridge for those who need to keep busy. I recommend childhood card games. They are not only simple, but by association they can bring our minds back to a time that was carefree. Buy specialty cards like Old Maid, Animal Rummy, or Crazy 8's and play with your children, spouse, friend, or borrow a niece, nephew, or neighborhood child. With a regular card deck you can play silly games like Go Fish, Slap Jack, or Steal the Old Man's Pack. (Avoid serious competitive games like Hearts, Pinochle, or Bridge.)

✦

THE SEARCH FOR MEANING

Task H—Belief Continuums

In sorting out our beliefs we need to look at where we stand on four core issues. How much control does each person have over their destiny? What makes us who we are—environment or genetics? Are we born good or evil? Are we simply living organisms that are born and die without any rhyme or reason, or are we spiritual beings that have purpose, whose lives have meaning? Where would you place yourself on the continuums below?
Place an X on each line to indicate where you stand.

Born GOOD --Born EVIL

ANIMAL nature --SPIRITUAL being

FREEWILL --PREDESTINATION

ENVIRONMENT --GENETICS

ECONOMIC DETERMINISM ---------------------OPPORTUNITY REIGNS

SELF-CONTROL --------------------------------SUPERNATURAL CONTROL

INDIVIDUAL CHOICE ------------------------------EXTERNAL CONTROL

DIVERSITY --UNIFORMITY

✦

Part III:
On-Going Step Work

For the categories listed below, please refer to the explanations given in the introduction. Remember, this is your journal to use as you wish.

✦ 1. Stories of others that have helped me see myself.

✦ 1. Stories of others that have helped me see myself. *(Continued)*

✦ 2. **Relevant dreams.** What did you learn this month by opening yourself up to messages from your unconscious?

✦ 2. Relevant dreams. *(Continued)*

✦ 3. Confessions.

✦ 3. Confessions. *(Continued)*

✦ 4. Small Achievements and Stepping Stones.

✦ 5. Conflicts and their resolution or non-resolution. Who or what have I tried to control this month?

✦ 5. Conflicts and their resolution or non-resolution. *(Continued)*

✦ 5. Conflicts and their resolution or non-resolution. *(Continued)*

✦ 6. Reflections. (Date each entry)

✦ 6. Reflections. *(Continued)*

✦ 6. Reflections. *(Continued)*

✦ 6. Reflections. *(Continued)*

✦ 6. Reflections. *(Continued)*

STEP 3

We made a decision to let go of control, assume a spirit of goodwill, seek the wisdom of responsible others, and discover our true "voice within."

Part I: The Meaning of Step 3[1]

Addicted people and co-dependents are usually compulsive. Compulsions, or uncontrollable urges to act in certain patterned ways, take hold when we are psychologically "stuck." In response to stress we often fall back on old patterns, or do what has worked in the past because change causes anxiety. We stick to the same ways of doing things in spite of the fact that life changes all around us. We grow older, our children grow older, new co-workers replace old ones, our health and energy levels change, new roads are built, new restaurants open. But we persist with the tried and true, ignoring how much our world has changed, because we know only what has worked in the past.

Step 3 signals a time for change. Compulsive people fall in love with their ruts. They become convinced that their way is the best way. It's all they know how to do.

Whether in a position of leadership where we can order everyone else to do things our way, or as a side-line curmudgeon who sabotages any new approaches, we keep control by blocking

1. You may wish to read Melody Beattie *Codependent No More* (Harper & Row, 1987).

change. We cannot trust things to turn out well if there is any variation from our plan.

This is what we must change.

Compulsive people overburden themselves by trying to run or control everything. They operate from a basic belief that the whole world will fall apart if they turn their attention away for a minute. Some do this out of an exaggerated sense of their own power and indispensability, while others feel so out-of-control that they compensate by struggling to gain a sense of power.

We need to learn to trust something beyond ourselves. Some turn to God; modern pragmatists look for strength in a variety of sources. Even if we were more intelligent and experienced than all our co-workers or the others on our committee, does that mean we can do the job better than all of them combined? It is not only egomaniacal to believe that, it is also unmathematical. Each of our days has twenty-four hours. Each of our ten committee members has twenty-four hours in each of their days. Can we really believe that we can do more in twenty-four hours than they can do in their combined 240 hours?

If we listen to those around us, instead of silencing them with a barrage of our words, we will learn new ideas. We do not know more than the combined wisdom of everyone we know. Perhaps no one person can tell us what we must do to change our unhappy lives, but, if we listen, the knowledge of several people may combine to form a whole plan that will support the changes we need to make.

We need to begin to believe that there are good ideas, solutions, help, and support out there ready for the taking. We need to acquire the humility to let go of some of our own ideas and see what happens when we let others try out their ideas. We need to believe that no matter how brilliant we are, we do not know *everything* and even the simplest player may have just the answer we need right now.

Even when we have the best solution, we cannot expect others to help us carry it out if it is in the form of an order given from the top. When our co-workers, friends, or families have not felt heard, they are likely to resist. One cannot be a leader without followers. If our arrogance is replaced by humility, others will take our ideas as seriously as we take theirs. It is wise to seek consensus in all your dealings with others.

When we stop trying to control, when we trust life to go on without our constant vigilant attention, time opens up for us. At this stage in our recovery we need to learn to relax by new, more healthy means. We need time for reflection. We need to think over the ideas others have given us and seriously consider how well they might work for us. At the same time, we need to seek our own better judgment in the words of that still small voice within. We have all known moments when we discovered we knew the solution to our problem all along, if only we had stopped to think about what we were doing and what the consequences might be. When we take the time for reflection, we instinctively know what is good for us and what is bad for us.

Set aside time each day for meditation, journal writing, reading brief wisdom aphorisms—whatever calms you enough to be able to hear that voice within. Stop flying by the seat of your pants and live a more carefully considered life. When things don't turn out exactly as you planned, consider what can be learned from the incident. Is there some surprising positive result? Remember, no life is without struggle or pain. It is what we do with that pain that matters.

Climb out of your own ego enough to see that each person around you is struggling with his or her own problems, trying to bring life in line with his or her own vision. When they thwart your plans, it is rarely out of malice. More often it is just a happenstance of them following their own star and stepping on you as they speed past. Don't waste time on resentment. Shake it off and continue on your journey.

✦

Part II: Workbook Section on Step 3

Do these in whatever order suits you.

Task A—Control Issue

1. What things, people, or circumstances have you tried to control in the past?

2. What are your worst fears about giving up control? Think of a task before you that requires you to work with others (or analyze one that happened recently).

If you sat back and decided to be a follower this time what is the worst thing that could happen?

What is the best thing that could happen?

What would have happened if you were in charge?

What would be the *likely* outcome if someone else took over?

✦

Task B—Trusting a Sponsor

Most programs suggest that you select a person you feel has some wisdom and will be supportive of you, and then ask for his or her help. If you are in a Twelve Step program, it is wise to choose someone who has been in the program for a number of years. If not, sometimes a colleague, old friend, or therapist will do.

Who are you considering for a sponsor? It is strongly recommended that, if you are heterosexual, you choose someone of the same sex as yourself, and if you are gay or lesbian, you chose someone of the opposite sex. At such a vulnerable time it is too easy to become sexually involved with a sponsor who might be attractive to you.

List five possibilities with their phone numbers. Call each one up just to chat. Then rank order them according to whom you think would be best for you:

Name	Phone	Rank

You may want to sit on this decision for a while and see if time bears out your initial judgment. Then, when you feel ready, reach out!

✦

Task C—Triggers

What events or circumstances trigger cravings or have caused you to lose your resolve in the past?

Hunger? Food? Post-caffeine or post-sugar slump? Anxiety?
Fatigue? Traffic? Deadlines? Conflict? Loss?
Disappointment? Boss? A particular difficult person? Parties?
Endings? Beginnings? Celebrations? Holidays?

Circle all of the above that apply and write in others.

____

____

What alternative behavior can you substitute for your addiction? Juice instead of alcohol? A nap instead of blowing up? A good exit line in too-tempting circumstances? Be specific. Exercise? Sex? Creative outlet? Bath or shower? Meditation? Play with a child or a pet?

Trigger **Solution**

______________________ ______________________________________

______________________ ______________________________________

______________________ ______________________________________

______________________ ______________________________________

______________________ ______________________________________

Which crises can be prevented by some preplanning, such as bringing your own nonalcoholic drink to a party, getting eight hours sleep each night, anticipating problems with others . . . (think of your own).

______________________ ______________________________________

______________________ ______________________________________

✦

Task D—Methods

What methods will you use to keep your addiction in check? Check all that apply and elaborate on one or two below:

_____ abstinence

_____ writing

_____ telephone

_____ service to others

_____ meditation

_____ Twelve Step meetings

_____ reading

_____ sponsor

_____ therapy

_____ exercise

____

____

____

____

✦

BREATHER!

Task E—Pleasure

Check the things that give you pleasure and schedule at least one per week for the next month.

______ fancy dinner out	______ fancy dinner in
______ movie on big screen	______ a novel
______ cards or board games	______ dancing
______ special company	______ coffee with friend
______ new clothing	______ massage
______ steam room or sauna	______ frozen yogurt
______ jigsaw puzzle	______ crafts or drawing
other ______________________	______________________
______________________	______________________
______________________	______________________

Make a commitment by selecting an activity per week:

Week 1 ______________________	Week 2 ______________________
Week 3 ______________________	Week 4 ______________________

✦

Task F—Developing Humility

Humility is not obsequious self-flagellation. It is simply admitting that you are not God, and that there may be some things that you do not do better than everyone else. (Some would call this facing reality.) Humility may also be actions taken without regard to pride. Plan to do some good things for which you will not get credit.

List three secret good deeds you have done or plan to do (perhaps you could help someone else accomplish *their* goal):

1. ______________________________
2. ______________________________
3. ______________________________

Attend a meeting or gathering where you are normally a big talker and just listen.

Meeting & Date **Result**

______________ ______________________

____

____

✦

Task G—Health Plan

Addictions leave us drained and unhealthy. We forget to eat or eat whatever is handy regardless of its nutritional value. We are generally too busy or unmotivated for any kind of exercise on a regular basis. A depleted body will undermine our efforts to overcome our addiction. Poor health effects our mood and endurance. We need to plan and follow a good diet and get regular exercise to help us accomplish our goal of abstinence.

DIET: Decide three unhealthy eating habits you will give up:

1. ______________________________
2. ______________________________
3. ______________________________

Select three healthy food habits you plan to begin.

1. ______________________________
2. ______________________________
3. ______________________________

EXERCISE: Depending on your current physical health, your exercise plan may be something as simple as a walk around the block three times a week or as complex as a weight training and aerobic routine at a health club. Try to select something to which you can look forward. (I go on long hikes with my very enthusiastic dog.)
My exercise plan for this month:

____

____

____

Date I will begin: ______________________________

✦

Task H—Relaxation Suggestion

Draw yourself a nice warm bath and put on some music that always lightens your mood. If it's winter, bring a nice hot cup of herbal tea to the bath; if summer, fix a tall, cool lemonade. Some find bubbles wonderful, others like moisturizing beads. Men may want to sprinkle aftershave into the water. If you would rather take a shower, turn up the music loud and sing along. Let the shower run a good long time, moving your body slowly through the water to help the stream massage your neck, back, shoulders, lower back, etc.

✦

SEARCH FOR MEANING

Task I—Five Basic Questions

To determine what our values and beliefs are, we should ask ourselves five basic questions: 1) Who am I? For what do I feel responsible? Of what do I feel capable? 2) What do I trust? Do I follow people in authority, the knowledge in books, or my own personal experience? 3) Where can I find meaning?

In a church, in nature, with people, in fantasy? 4) How shall I live? What is my code of ethics? What do I believe is a good use of my time? 5) What happens after I die?

Who am I? ____

What do I trust? ____________________________________

Where can I find meaning? _____________________________

How shall I live? ___________________________________

What happens after I die? _____________________________

✦

Elaborate on one of these issues here:

Part III: On-Going Step Work

For the categories listed below, please refer to the explanations given in the introduction. Feel free to skip around or save some for later. You are in charge of this journal.

✦ 1. Stories of others that have helped me see myself.

✦ 1. Stories of others that have helped me see myself *(Continued)*

✦ 2. Relevant dreams.

✦ 2. Relevant dreams *(Continued)*

✦ 3. Confessions.

✦ 3. Confessions *(Continued)*

✦ 4. Small Achievements and Stepping Stones.
Was I able to give up control of anything this month?

✦ 5. Conflicts and their resolution or nonresolution.

✦ 5. Conflicts and their resolution or nonresolution *(Continued)*

✦ 5. Conflicts and their resolution or nonresolution *(Continued)*

✦ 6. Reflections. (Date each entry)
Is my still small voice within becoming clearer to me?

✦ 6. Reflections. *(Continued)*

✦ 6. Reflections. *(Continued)*

✦ 6. Reflections. *(Continued)*

✦ 6. Reflections. *(Continued)*

STEP 4

We made a searching and fearless inventory of our strengths and weaknesses.

Part I: The Meaning of Step 4[1]

We cannot change for the better until we have a thorough understanding of our own strengths and weaknesses. Though many of us have become beaten down to the point that we aren't sure we have any strengths, we are even more reluctant to list our weaknesses. As soon as we attempt to bring our weaknesses to mind, the weaknesses of others seem far more glaring.

If we have grown up in an alcoholic or otherwise dysfunctional home we have probably received a great deal of mistreatment and are very aware of the faults of our parents. If we have been living with an addiction of our own for awhile and have reached the point of wanting to change, it is probably because we've been mistreated and disappointed by our current group of cronies. We can be so preoccupied with the wrongs others have committed against us that we can forget that it takes two to make a conflict. We may not have initiated the wrongs, but if we continue to stew about them and there is an atmosphere of mutual animosity, then we have either failed to do our part to end the conflict (passive-resistance), or we have taken small subtle measures to keep the bad feelings alive.

The most frequent and troublesome faults found in those living

---

1. You may wish to read Harold H. Bloomfield and Leonard Felder, *Making Peace With Your Parents* (New York: Ballantine Books, 1983).

with an addiction are self-righteousness, rationalizations, grudge-bearing, retaliation (or revenge), oversensitivity, and resentment. If we tend more toward self-pity than self-righteousness, we may also be filled with guilt and remorse. These are all poisonous feelings that lead to alienation and depression.

Through these feelings we experience the truth of the old adage, "Hate hurts the hater far more than the hated." Our self-righteousness causes us to be hypercritical of others while blocking knowledge of any constructive changes we need to make in ourselves. By denying all our faults and focusing on the faults of others, we set ourselves outside the ring of humanity, for no one can bear to be friends with someone who so lacks humility.

When we rationalize every wrong we commit, we fail to learn from our mistakes and are doomed to repeat the behaviors that keep us from getting close to others or finding peace of mind. When we bear grudges, every little wrong becomes a major crime or personal affront that we pledge to never forget. We lose our ability to accept apologies and put our hurts behind us. Every small conflict escalates to a war. By retaliating or seeking revenge we push the conflict to the point of no return. It can take years to unravel a series of hurts and retaliations. And yet the conflict could have been contained and ended at any point, if just one person had been willing *not* to retaliate.

Oversensitivity and resentment often go hand in hand. While believing in their own innocence, the overly sensitive sometimes keep scorecards on their every slight. On the surface, they look like victims, but anyone who has tried to avoid hurting an oversensitive person soon discovers they have been cast in the role of persecutor. Every neutral remark may be translated into a criticism by the overly sensitive and serves to close them up in a cage of misery. The problem lies in their perception: even when an insult is intended, they could turn it into a compliment with a smart quip and let it drift off harmlessly into the atmosphere. But too often they grab it and thrust it into their hearts. They don't realize that they have that *choice* every time.

But the most serious and all pervasive trait of various addicts and those who live with addiction is *resentment*. Far more powerful than anger, it hides and festers. Someone asks us for a favor. It is inconvenient, but we smile and say yes. It creates pressure and chaos for us, and we do it with hate in our hearts, thinking all the while that they were inconsiderate to ask. Are we everyone's slave? Yes. And if we haven't got the courage to say no, we should be happy slaves. We cannot expect others to read our minds, to know that when we say yes, we really mean no. Unlike grudges, which are usually accompanied by a specific list of wrongs that could theoretically be forgiven someday, resentment is an all pervasive feeling or life attitude that seeps into everything.

The point of Step 4 is to begin to discover why things keep going wrong in our lives. We need to discover what we alone can change in ourselves to reverse a trend of unhappiness, because we can only change ourselves.

Have we had a series of broken friendships? Have they hurt us and we couldn't forgive? Have we responded to every slight with retaliation and held a grudge all out of proportion with the crime? Is it a question of pride over who should apologize first? Do we adhere to some rigid code of conduct that our friends have unknowingly violated (like not returning an invitation to dinner)?

Every unresolved conflict creates noise in our brain that obliterates our peace of mind. The scenes replay and replay in our minds while we experience guilt or remorse or anger over what we think we *should* have done. These grudges keep us frozen in our development. When we fail to resolve this conflict, no other conflict will be worked through beyond this point. It holds the key to the next step.

✦

Part II:
Workbook Section on Step 4

Note: This searching and fearless inventory is for your eyes only. This step can be very challenging. Take as much time as you need. If you find these tasks too overwhelming, chip away at them a little each day.

Task A—The Poisonous Ones

Few of us have escaped the poisonous attitudes below. Press yourself to remember or acknowledge when you have used these tactics or shown these traits. Specify when, how, and with whom:

Self-righteousness ______________________________

____

____

Rationalizations ______________________________

____

____

Grudge-bearing ______________________________

____

____

Retaliation (revenge) ______________________________

____

____

Oversensitivity ____

____

____

Resentment ____

____

____

✦

Task B—Weaknesses

Even when we mean to confess our weaknesses, we may have trouble calling them to mind. We know we are not perfect, but what exactly are *our* faults? It sometimes helps to think about the traits we hate most in others (because they are often our own shortcomings) or to consider how we are like our mothers or fathers. That, and a long list to choose from, should get you going.

Possible faults: selfish, dishonest, cowardly, fearful, controlling, manipulative, intimidating, power-hungry, possessive, prejudiced, bigoted, an attention-grabber, greedy, materialistic, snobbish, sarcastic, hypercritical, gossiper, spendthrift, blamer, harsh, unforgiving, verbally abusive, physically abusive, sexually abusive, impatient, lazy, a procrastinator, overly dependent, judgmental, overly preoccupied with sex, sexually selfish, adulterous, sneaky, cheater, liar, ungrateful, cynical, intolerant, self-pitying, bitter, rageful, jealous, envious, insecure

Choose those that fit and briefly describe how and when you have seen these traits in yourself.

Trait	Circumstances
______________	______________________________
______________	______________________________
______________	______________________________
______________	______________________________
______________	______________________________
______________	______________________________
______________	______________________________
______________	______________________________
______________	______________________________
______________	______________________________

✦

Task C—Acts of omission

If we have a passive personality, it is often the things that we do *not* do that make us so annoying to others and prolong our own misery. Do you relate to any of these? Place a check by those you practice:

______ worrying instead of doing
______ isolating yourself instead of reaching out
______ waiting for others to act first
______ hooking up with abusive people
______ holding onto destructive relationships
______ staying in a dead-end job
______ not expressing your feelings
______ dealing with conflict by avoidance
______ standing by while someone else is hurt
______ letting someone else get blamed for your actions
______ neglecting or abandoning someone dependent on you

✦

BREATHER!

Task D—Capturing Our Strengths

Claim all of these you can and list your top ten: generous, warm, kind, dependable, responsible, attractive, fun-loving, amusing, dedicated, hard-working, gentle, open, loving, affectionate, accepting, thrifty, forgiving, supportive, good mom, good dad, good friend, patient, industrious, efficient, honest, appreciative, tolerant, brave, even-tempered, intelligent, resourceful, helpful, compassionate, creative, talented, witty, welcoming, enthusiastic. And any others that apply to you.

✦

Task E—Fears

What are my fears? How have they caused me trouble throughout my life? How have my fears interfered with my happiness lately?

✦

Task F—Guilt, Shame and Remorse

How are my relations with my co-workers, friends, or neighbors? Have I stirred up conflict and left it unresolved? Is there something I wish I could do over differently?

How are my relations with my family of origin? Am I in conflict with any of my siblings? Are there bad feelings between me and my parents? Am I avoiding the whole issue?

Describe your major family themes and your part in any conflict:

How are my relations with my nuclear family? Are my spouse and I engaged in a cold war? Have I neglected or hurt my children? Is there anything I wish I could erase from my life?

✦

Task G—Changes

What three changes do I need to make first? How will these help me make amends?

1. ____

____

2. ____

____

3. ____

____

✦

Task H—Relaxation Suggestion

Browse your local library, bookstore, or record shop for tapes or CDs of nature sounds. Sounds of the ocean, gentle rainstorms, birds, or autumn winds can take you out into nature as you lie on your couch at the end of the day. If you grew up in the humid east and now live in the desert, the sounds of a rainstorm may remind you of better days. The sound of the ocean may transport you to romantic days by the sea. Some nature sound tapes mix in classical music. If you are one who has particular trouble "wasting time" you might try tapes that provide subliminal messages that promote positive thinking and other good habits while you lie there.

✦

SEARCH FOR MEANING

Task I—Process Theology

One school of thought asserts that our belief systems are formed and influenced by our life experiences. Important transitions, events, and crises teach us what kind of world we live in and form our philosophies of life. By answering the questions below you will begin to see what factors have determined your beliefs so that you can then decide if you want to allow these things to have the power of influence.

1. Time line—How much of your life have you used up already? Date the ends of the time line and then place an X on the point of the present.

________ ____ ________

Birth Death

2. Name three people who have had a tremendous impact on your life. In what way have they each influenced you?

a. __________ ____

Name Influence

____

b. __________ ____

____

c. __________ ____

____

3. Tell three experiences you had that changed you and describe how they changed you.

a. ____

____

b. ____

____

c. ____

____

4. What decisions have you made in your life that had a significant impact on the course of your life? How did you go about making those decisions?

____

____

____

____

____

5. Where would you place the above factors on your time line? Do you see any kind of pattern?

____

____

✦

Part III: On-Going Step Work

For the categories listed below, please refer to the explanations given in the introduction. You may find subjects in the short answer tasks that you'd like to explore more fully here.

✦ 1. Stories of others that have helped me see myself.

Is there a person I hate who shows me the trait I most dislike in myself?

✦ 1. Stories of others that have helped me see myself. *(Continued)*

✦ 2. Relevant dreams. When I see myself in my dreams, am I the same kind of person that I am in my waking life? If not, who is the *real* me?

✦ 2. Relevant dreams. *(Continued)*

✦ 3. Confessions.

✦ 3. Confessions. *(Continued)*

✦ 4. Small Achievements and Stepping Stones. (Brief descriptions.)

✦ 5. Conflicts and their resolution or nonresolution.

✦ 5. Conflicts and their resolution or nonresolution. *(Continued)*

✦ 5. Conflicts and their resolution or nonresolution. *(Continued)*

✦ 6. Reflections. (Date each entry)

✦ 6. Reflections. *(Continued)*

✦ 6. Reflections. *(Continued)*

✦ 6. Reflections. *(Continued)*

✦ 6. Reflections. *(Continued)*

STEP 5

We admitted to our journal, ourselves, and to another human being the exact nature of our wrongs.

Part I: The Meaning of Step 5[1]

We all experience duality to some degree. Many of us are one type of personality at the office and someone different at home. We are one kind of person with children and someone entirely different at the bar. We may behave in certain ways with someone we are dating that would make us unrecognizable to our best friends. In small amounts and for brief periods of time this duality is normal and harmless.

But if we have become addicted or lived with addiction we are likely to experience much stronger personality differences when in various situations. If the damage has gone on long enough, we begin to feel like Dr. Jekyll and Mr. Hyde. To keep our jobs and public respect, we act our best in the light of day outside our home. But this can become a tremendous strain, and the tension it produces is often taken out on the people we live with. We cannot keep up the charade twenty-four hours a day.

As our addiction deepens, the pressure from our "dark side" intensifies and our worst selves begin to spill over into other areas of our lives. Some of us openly show our hostility, certain in our own self-righteousness that our actions are well-deserved. Others find that their dark thoughts and petty attitudes embarrass them when they

1. You may wish to read Sam Keen and Anne Valley-Fox, *Your Mythic Journey* (Los Angeles: Jeremy P. Tarcher, 1989).

emerge, tarnishing the Mr. or Ms. Nice Guy facade we'd been projecting.

Some of us have led double lives for years. We may have a whole separate set of friends—our drinking cronies. We might be a proper schoolteacher by day and a sex addict at night. We may tell ourselves that because we have to be such a stuffed shirt at work that we need a little something to loosen us up at night. Sometimes the activities of our "shadow" become so atrocious and embarrassing to us that we block them out totally. We have blackouts when we cannot remember anything we did for a twenty-four-hour period. Sometimes we have done truly shameful things, and sometimes there is no one to tell us what we did. We worry how far we would actually go. Have we stolen, raped, or murdered?

Many of us go to therapy and lie our way through the session. We can't bear to have anyone know about our promiscuity, temper tantrums, mean-spiritedness, poisonous envy, or disloyalty. We pray that no one will discover the truth about our lies or fabrications of success. We dread the thought that our children or co-workers may have seen us passed out or puking out our guts. We may have many many shameful secrets that we have kept from our spouses.

What is unspeakable is highly personalized. For very sensitive people the dread might be that we feel we have deceived others about who we really are. We imagine ourselves to be dull, incompetent, or desperately insecure while we project a facade of success at work. We smile when we want to cry. We remain aloof when we want to cling. We spend enormous sums on clothes and makeup trying to compensate for our feelings of unattractiveness. We have no close friends because we dread they will find out who we *really* are and reject us.

And yet, before we can feel whole and healed, we will have to speak the unspeakable. First, by recording the events in our journal, then by telling ourselves aloud on a mountaintop, or before a mirror, and then by telling one other trusted person. In order to overcome our sense of alienation, in order to rejoin the human race, we have to risk being truly known and hope that we will be accepted despite our faults. When we try being honest, we usually find out that others don't view us as harshly as we view ourselves.

First we select a trustworthy person. If we are in a Twelve Step group, a sponsor or anyone else who has completed Step 5 themselves may serve as a good listener. If not, we may go to a clergy person, therapist, or other professional who has had experience with listening to other's dark secrets. We may want to confide in a close friend. This can be wonderful as long as we can trust his or her total confidentiality and as long as we have not committed crimes against him or her.

The person we choose must be neutral and unaffected by our transgressions. Usually this makes it impossible to confess to a spouse or parent or another with whom we have been in a close relationship for years. Later we will make amends. For now we are just seeking unconditional acceptance for ourselves, regardless of our shortcomings and mistakes. It takes quite a special person to give that kind of acceptance.

We want our listener to listen without judging or trying to fix us. We don't want advice at this point. We may want to give them instructions about how we need them to listen. For example, we may know that we will never manage to get through our whole list if they offer comments or dialogue along the way, so we may want to tell them not to interrupt. Others may need to ask for ongoing reassurance so that they do not feel "judged" by the silence.

We want to make sure that we have a safe place to share our confidences. We may want to sit outdoors somewhere, far from phones or human traffic. If we meet indoors, we need to request that there be no distractions allowed. Turn off the radio, the TV, and the phone and agree not to answer the door.

Once safe, we launch into our narrative. We may want to write it all out beforehand to make sure we forget nothing. This will not just be a recitation of events. We will share our motives, thoughts, and rationalizations at the time of our "crime." We need to tell how we felt about it then and how we feel about it now. We need to remember what consequences we and others suffered from our actions. What in our nature caused us to do it? What has been the long term effect of carrying these negative feelings and shameful secrets? We want to strip away everything, reveal all our best tricks, so that we can no longer fool ourselves in the future.

When we are done, we suddenly feel a part of the human race again.

✦

Part II: Workbook Section on Step 5

(Keep in mind that the more you open up in your journal, the easier it will be to open up to another human being. This is your chance to rehearse and reflect before you take this big step.)

✦

Task A—Patterns

Look back at your answers and lists in Step 4. Do you see any patterns emerging? Let these guide you toward putting your confession in some order. Outline what you want to talk about below. Be sure to include a section on sex or money. These are subjects we shy away from, but often our most shameful memories are connected to our sexuality or our spending habits. Clear yourself of bad feelings on these issues by being open and honest about them now.

1. ______________________________

____

____

2. ______________________________

____

____

3. ______________________________

____

____

4. Sex and/or Money ____

____

____

____

✦

Task B—Deceit

What did you do to conceal your liquor, food, sex, or drug consumption? What other deceptions did this lead to?

____

____

____

____

✦

Task C—Limitations and Capabilities

What does all of the above reveal to you about your limitations and capabilities? Name 5 of each.

Limitations	**Capabilities**
______________	______________
______________	______________
______________	______________
______________	______________
______________	______________

✦

BREATHER!

Task D—Strengths Behind Weaknesses

Often a potential strength lurks behind a more obvious weakness. A fault may just be too much of a good thing. Circle the pairs of characteristics below that seem to apply to you.

irresponsible/playful
aloof/self-reliant
overly sensitive/empathic
unrealistic/imaginative
super responsible/dependable
clingy/affectionate
self-indulgent/generous
rigidity/consistency

Add some pairs that are not on the list. See if you can find the strengths behind your greatest weaknesses.

___

___

___

✦

Task E—Who Am I?

Home personality ___

___

___

___

Work/school personality ___

___

___

___

My hidden self ______________________________

____

____

____

✦

Task F—Deepest Secrets

What is just too shameful to tell? Why?

____

____

____

Whom will it hurt if I tell it? ______________________________

____

✦

Task G—My Confidant

What characteristics do I want my confidant to have? Male? Female? Warm? Reserved? Talkative? Quiet? Clergy person? Therapist? Friend? It is better to avoid someone with whom you have day-to-day contact, such as a family member or co-worker. Remember to select a same-sex, or opposite-sex listener, whichever is appropriate, to avoid mucking up the experience with sexual feelings.

____

____

____

Who do I know with these characteristics?

____________________ ____________________ ____________________

Note: Who you share your inventory with is very important to the success of this step. If there is no one in your present circle who seems appropriate, it is okay to postpone this part of the step, as long as you are willing to proceed when the right person is available. However, there is no need to delay telling your journal and yourself. You might also consider telling these things to a therapist.

✦

Task H—Your Fearless Inventory of Strengths and Weaknesses

Using the material in the above exercises as well as those in Step 4, write out your inventory as you would tell it to someone else. You may want to write it in chronological order or organize it by categories of strengths and weaknesses. You may want to begin with the things you are proud of and work your way down to your worst transgressions. When you are done, reward yourself with some pleasurable activity. Take a hot bath, watch a movie or ball game, or go to dinner with a good friend.

✦

Task I—Relaxation Suggestion

Lonely? Games can relax you while taking the sting out of an evening without company. There are many methods of playing Solitare. Check out a game book and learn a new way to play cards with yourself. You might also like to try computer games. Travel through the United States with Carmen SanDiego and solve a mystery, or build a city of the future with Sim City software. Explore a castle, invent a machine, or "chat" with someone who shares your on-line service. Play is as essential to your well-being as is sleep or nutritious food.

✦

SEARCH FOR MEANING

Task J—Your Personal Myth

Are there any fairy tales, myths, or fables that struck a familiar chord in you? Using one of these as a base, or starting from scratch, outline the myth of your life. Who is the hero or heroine of your myth? Who or what was the obstacle you had to overcome? What tasks did you have to carry out? Were there any magical moments? Write several endings and then choose one for which to aim. You might want to refer back to your time line in Chapter 4.

Once upon a time ______________________________

____

____

____

____

✦

Part III:
On-Going Step Work

(This is a very intense step. The previous exercises have probably caused you to do some serious soul-searching. You may want to finish this step out with more upbeat reflections: funny stories, pleasant dreams, small step forward. Be gentle on yourself here. You've reached a difficult step.)

For the categories listed below, please refer to the explanations given in the introduction.

✦ 1. Stories of others that have helped me see myself.

✦ 1. Stories of others that have helped me see myself. *(Continued)*

✦ 2. Relevant dreams.

✦ 2. Relevant dreams. *(Continued)*

✦ 3. Confessions. You may have some highly personal and specific things you'd like to get off your chest here. Remember, all that is truly repented is forgiven.

✦ 3. Confessions. *(Continued)*

✦ 4. Small Achievements and Stepping Stones. (Brief descriptions.)

✦ 5. Conflicts and their resolution or nonresolution.

✦ 5. Conflicts and their resolution or nonresolution. *(Continued)*

✦ 5. Conflicts and their resolution or nonresolution. *(Continued)*

✦ 6. Reflections. (Date each entry)

✦ 6. Reflections. *(Continued)*

✦ 6. Reflections. *(Continued)*

✦ 6. Reflections. *(Continued)*

✦ 6. Reflections. *(Continued)*

STEP 6

Were entirely ready to listen to wise counsel and seek that still small voice within to guide us to change our behaviors which have been harmful to ourselves and others.

Part I: The Meaning of Step 6[1]

Change is difficult. Our natural instinct is to resist change. We will go to great lengths to try and change everything and everyone around us before we will consider changing ourselves. But being "entirely ready" means that we have declared our willingness to change.

What has brought us to this point? People generally won't agree to change unless they are suffering terrible consequences from remaining the same. Addicts, who are frequently compulsive and rigid, are especially resistant. But in today's complex and fast-changing society, we need to be flexible in order to survive.

In addition to our own reluctance, we must overcome all the resistant pressure being applied by others in our environments. In each group to which we belong—family, workplace, circle of friends—a comfortable pattern of interaction has been established. We each fall into natural roles in response to one another. We sense we are to play straight man to someone else's jokes, or that we are seen as the "radical feminist" of the group and the other's are counting on

1. You may wish to read Martin E. P. Seligman, *What You Can Change and What You Can't* (New York: Knopf, 1993).

us for feminist chastisements when anyone uses words like "mankind."

There are many levels of roles we play in our groups, and they are all in perfect balance until someone decides to change. The "routine" then no longer works, and everyone fears that they will have to change, too. When we begin to clean up our acts, our coworkers may suddenly start worrying that we might be competing for their jobs. Our drinking friends will be very threatened by our not drinking. Even our families may not welcome our changes. For as much as they might have complained, they have also become comfortable in their roles of rescuer, persecutor, or parentified child. When we try to take back our proper place in the family, others may start to panic.

Any of these people, as a result of their own fears or discomfort, may try to undermine our change by getting us addicted again. So our resolve must be very strong.

This is probably why many addicts must "hit bottom" first. The effects of not changing must be very painful before we will want to put forth the tremendous effort required for change. As we look over our lists of faults and weaknesses and remember the anxiety they have caused us in the past, we believe that we would welcome change. Who wouldn't want to stop passing out on concrete sidewalks?

But the subtle difficulty with this step comes from the demand that we change all defects of character, even if we *benefit* from them. For example, say we have a cabinet-making business. We know if we hang the doors off-kilter the customer will complain, refuse to pay us, report us to the Better Business Bureau, and tell all his friends not to hire us. So we want to be sober enough to hang the doors straight. But, if we clear a nice tidy profit by using cheap materials that only last five years instead of twenty years, and which initially look as good as the better quality wood, do we want to feel so compelled to be honest that we tell the customer what they are really getting?

We not only benefit from some of our defects of character, we love them, depend on them, and see them as necessary tools of survival. We love feeling superior. We love piling up money and goods. Gossiping is fun. False pride, arrogance, and self-righteousness can be good substitutes for a deficit in self-esteem. We may worry that by giving up cynicism, we will leave ourselves wide open for injury. Our defects often form a protective shell around us. Will we be so willing to give these up?

That is the true challenge of Step 6.

We'd really like to have the bad *consequences* of the defects removed and still keep the defects. We prefer others to stop reacting to our bad behaviors in ways that cause us grief. Until we can convince ourselves that the defects cost us more than they give, we will not be ready. We must have an alternative in mind that has greater appeal before we'll be motivated to change.

For example, if my petty jealousy of my sister and my clever put downs of her have gained me the admiration of my other siblings, in order to stop, I would need to believe that either my sibs can admire me for other things, or that I might gain a warm close relationship with my sister by publicly supporting her achievements. Punishment has never been the best motivator; the promise of reward is far more effective.

It is easiest to begin with the defects that are causing us the most trouble. When we have cleared one away and have felt the gratitude and self-appreciation for the change accomplished, we will have a greater willingness to change another defect. Eventually we will no longer be motivated only by the avoidance of punishment. We will be able to understand the quiet satisfaction of doing a good job or giving others pleasure. We need positives like this to motivate us to change the things we recognize are wrong, even when they feel so right.

We don't want to rush ourselves, like a hothouse plant that has been pushed to bloom too soon and shortly dies of exhaustion. Our defects serve a purpose, like poles propping up a tent. If we remove one without first putting a compensating prop in its place, the tent will come down around us. That's why in AA they say, "Easy does it," and "Let's take it one day at a time."

Meditate. Reflect. Slow your life down. Take the time to develop a nonjudgmental awareness of yourself, and listen to the advice of others. Accept yourself as fallible, and be willing to accept help. Lean on your group for support and gentle criticism. Then let down your guard and open your heart. Have the faith that you can change all you need to change, in time.

✦

Part II: Workbook Section on Step 6

(Be sure to pace yourself gently.)

✦

Task A—The Seven Deadly Attitudes

Defects can be categorized under the following headings. In the space provided after each heading, record the specific ways you have given in to each deadly attitude.

PRIDE (Conceit or disdain for others)

____

____

GREED (Selfishness, materialism, nothing is enough)

____

____

LUST (Sexual indulgence without consideration for others)

____

____

DISHONESTY (Lying, cheating, defraud, deceit)

____

____

GLUTTONY (Covetousness, excessive eating, drinking, shopping)

____

____

ENVY (Jealousy, the desire to possess what others have)

____

____

LAZINESS (Procrastination, avoidance of responsibility)

____

____

✦

Task B—Defect Analysis

Begin by rank ordering your defects of character as you have discovered them in the last three chapters. In the second column, record what benefit you have received from this defect in the past. In the third column, record the problems this defect has caused you.

Defect	**Benefit**	**Problems**
EXAMPLE: dishonesty	more money	lost job and respect

✦

Task C—Plan to Overcome Defects

Repeat the above list and plan your strategy for change. In the second column, write what temptation might make you "slip" in your plan to halt this trait. Then in the third column, note your contingency plan. What positive alternative will you use as a substitute to keep from slipping?

Defect	**Temptation**	**Prevention**
EXAMPLE:		
dishonesty	*quick buck*	*call sponsor*
______	______	______
______	______	______
______	______	______
______	______	______
______	______	______
______	______	______
______	______	______
______	______	______
______	______	______
______	______	______

✦

BREATHER!

Task D—Positive Changes

What changes have you begun to notice in yourself? Are you thinking less defensively? Have you done any anonymous good deeds lately? How long have you been abstinent? Have you been spending more time with your loved ones? Let yourself feel well-earned pride, and brag about your progress below.

____

____

____

____

____

✦

Task E—More changes

What are you willing to change? Which defects will be the hardest to give up? List the specific defects of character you plan to tackle first, in the order you plan to tackle them.

1. ______________ 4. ______________
2. ______________ 5. ______________
3. ______________ 6. ______________

✦

Task F—Regression Plan

What kinds of stresses or pressures generally cause you to regress? What can you start to do right now that will lessen the likelihood of that stress occurring?

Stressor:

____

Ways to lessen impact:

Stressor:

Ways to lessen impact:

Stressor:

Ways to lessen impact:

✦

Task G—Support

To whom or to what can you turn for support during this challenging time?

Supportive People

Supportive Groups

Peaceful Places

______________________ ______________________

______________________ ______________________

Calming Activities

______________________ ______________________

______________________ ______________________

Fun!

______________________ ______________________

______________________ ______________________

✦

Task H—Relaxation Suggestion

Entertain yourself with a night at the movies. If you are tense, watch a comedy; if you're sad, watch a tearjerker that will help you shed bottled-up tears. If you are a worrier, watch an absorbing mystery; if you have a boring, uninspiring job, get intellectual stimulation from watching a classic film or an "art" film. If you are at home, be sure to take this time seriously by not answering the phone or allowing interruptions. Fix yourself a healthy treat within your calorie budget like popcorn or frozen yogurt, or splurge on brownies. If you haven't gotten out of the house much in a few days, go to a movie theater rather than watching a movie at home. You probably won't be the only one who has come to the theater alone, and the laughter of the crowd or the rustling around you will take the edge off your loneliness.

✦

SEARCH FOR MEANING

Task I—Hope

What do you say to reassure yourself during hard times? Do you have a special place you like to go when you are feeling troubled? Is there any person you know who makes you feel buoyant even on the worst of days? What makes you lose hope? What restores (or would restore) your hope or faith in humanity? What are your hopes for your future?

✦

Part III: On-Going Step Work

For the categories listed below, please refer to the explanations given in the introduction.

✦ 1. Stories of others that have helped me see myself.

✦ 1. Stories of others that have helped me see myself. *(Continued)*

✦ 2. **Relevant dreams.** Have your dreams revealed any feelings you've been trying to hide from yourself?

✦ 2. Relevant dreams. *(Continued)*

✦ 3. Confessions.

✦ 3. Confessions. *(Continued)*

✦ 4. Small Achievements and Stepping Stones. (Brief descriptions.)

✦ 5. Conflicts and their resolution or nonresolution.

✦ 5. Conflicts and their resolution or nonresolution. *(Continued)*

✦ 5. Conflicts and their resolution or nonresolution. *(Continued)*

✦ 6. **Reflections.** (Date each entry)

✦ 6. Reflections. *(Continued)*

✦ 6. Reflections. *(Continued)*

✦ 6. Reflections. *(Continued)*

✦ 6. Reflections. *(Continued)*

STEP 7

Humbly began the process of deep change so we could overcome our weaknesses.

Part I: The Meaning of Step 7[1]

Humility is a beautiful strengthening trait. An attitude of humility brings peace of mind, brings us closer to our true selves.

Humility is not *humiliation*. Humiliation destroys the self and brings endless mental suffering. Humility is an attitude we reach for within ourselves to open ourselves to learning and love. Humiliation is imposed on us by others who wish to destroy us. One is a self-given gift, the other a punishment from someone with a total lack of humility. Humility is having our feet on the ground, not having our face ground in the dirt!

Where there is no humility, there is arrogance and a total disregard for the feelings of others. But where there is humility, we find a deep respect for the self and others. As a nation we honor the rights of others to the "pursuit of happiness." For our founders knew that we are not gods, that we have no right to assume ourselves better than others, more worthy of life, or love, or success.

Humility is an equalizer. When we become humble, we understand our connection to all of humanity. A cut hurts each of us equally whether we are black, white, or Asian. We suffer the same pain

1. You may wish to read David Keirsey and Marilyn Bates, *Please Understand Me: Character and Temperament Types* (Del Mar, CA: Prometheus Nemesis Book Company, 1984).

whether we are rich or poor. We will bleed the same amount of blood whether we live in a mansion or a ghetto.

Humility opens doors. It teaches us to be tolerant of others' mistakes and view them with empathy. We become part of life again, rather than isolated from it by our false pride. We can learn from others by actively listening, where before our arrogance may have blocked our ears so we could not hear those younger than us, less educated than us, older than us, or less economically privileged than us. It opens all the wisdom of humanity to us.

Humility means letting go of the effort to control the uncontrollable. We can have serenity in the face of tragedy when we realize some things are simply beyond our control. We are not responsible for running the universe and anticipating every problem. Once we realize we do not have the power to change certain things, we can take them off our list of personal responsibilities. In this way, humility brings peace of mind.

Humility allows us to slow down our lives. We can give up the roles of superman or superwoman. We can admit that we just can't handle the overwhelming expectations aimed at today's adults. We don't have to wait until we are sick in bed to give ourselves a break. We can openly admit our limitations and downscale our lives to fit them. We can say to others, "All that activity was too much for me. I had to cut back." When we have humility, we are not afraid to reveal our limitations. We no longer need the status of being "in charge." We don't need to be president of the club, we can take our turn as a follower.

Before we achieved a spirit of humility, most of us had been making unreasonable demands on ourselves, others, and life itself. With such grand expectations, we were perpetually disappointed. If we lower our expectations and expect *nothing*, we will always be pleasantly surprised with whatever we do get. What were once disappointments will become reasons for joy.

How do we attain this sense of humility? By honestly admitting and examining our faults and relative strengths, we gain a more realistic sense of our limitations. As we strive to overcome our weaknesses, we must keep in mind that we are not trying to attain perfection. No one lives that long! Unfortunately, the more defects we tackle, the more we will see hiding underneath. We should not be discouraged, for our goal is not to be without faults, but rather to constantly improve ourselves. By realizing we have endless work to do on ourselves, we remain part of humanity, imperfect like all the rest. We belong.

To reach this state of peaceful self-understanding, we need to slow down our lives and make room for reflection. We need to cut back on commitments and minimize distractions. To initiate deep change it is wise to take time for solitude. Take a week off from work, cancel all plans, be sure you are alone so you will have time to think uninterrupted. Take back your life.

Reorganize your time so that you spend more time on the things that are positive and productive for you and with the people you love. Set a limit on how many hours you will work at your job. (Or if you have the opposite problem, strive for better attendance and do your part to support your work team.)

Shake off that conviction that the place will fall apart without you. As soon as you stop doing *everything*, others with talent will emerge to fill the gap. And as soon as you stop playing superservant at home, you will discover that even an eight-year-old can run a washer and dryer. Give up your position as an indispensable god and leave room for others to acquire some of your skills and knowledge. Become just one humble player on the team.

As we lighten our loads and create consistent times of reflection, we will be able to prevent the overwhelming build-up of problems. We can deal with things when they are small, anticipating as much as we can. With our time less rushed and our minds open and flexible we can hear when opportunity knocks. It will seem like a sudden onset of the miraculous once we have made time to listen to life. Everything we need is around us. We have only to take the time to stop and look.

✦

Part II: Workbook Section on Step 7

Task A—Rediscovering the True Self

Our temperaments and aptitudes are established in the womb. At birth, who we are begins to be influenced by the people and circumstances in our home. Were you a wiry extrovert born to a "quiet" family that exerted great energy to get you to quiet down? Or were you a bookish introvert forced to play contact sports? Think back to your earliest memories and describe who you were minus the influence of environment.

____

____

____

What forces may have masked or stifled your true self?

____

____

What would you like to recapture?

____

____

✦

Task B—Temperament

Reconnecting with who we are by nature helps us understand ourselves and our relations to others better. One of the best temperament tests is the Keirsey

Temperament Sorter[2] Personality types are assessed by evaluating them on four sets of variables:

Introvert vs. Extrovert: The introvert is drained by contact with people whereas the extrovert is energized under the same circumstances.

Sensation vs. Intuition: The sensor relies on touch, taste, sight, hearing, and smell and wants the facts. The intuiter relies more on the hypothetical.

Thinking vs. Feeling: The thinker prefers the objective and logical; the feeler prefers personal and value judgments.

Judging vs. Perceiving: Judgers want closure and hate unsettled business, while perceivers think there is never enough information to make a final decision and prefer to leave it open.

Where would you place yourself on the following scales?

Introvert ______________________________ Extrovert

Sensation ______________________________ Intuition

Thinking ______________________________ Feeling

Judging ______________________________ Perceiving

✦

Task C—The New You

Imagine yourself with your present defects of character removed. What will you be like?

____

____

____

✦

2. As published in Keirsey and Bates, *Please Understand Me.*

BREATHER!

Task D—Gifts of Grace

The atheist, knowing how fickle life is, probably has no trouble believing that "Shit Happens," as the bumper stickers say. Logically, we must also believe that Grace happens. When has "Providence" been good to you? What surprising good luck have you had? Do you feel grateful for good neighbors, good teachers, scholarships, natural talents, good health, attractiveness, fine grandparents, or a loyal pet? List your blessings below:

______________________ ______________________

______________________ ______________________

______________________ ______________________

______________________ ______________________

______________________ ______________________

✦

Task E—Priorities

Given twenty-four hours in a day, how many hours do you usually spend on the following in a typical day?

# of hours

SLEEP ______________________ ______

SCHOOL/MEETINGS ______________________ ______

WORK (earning money) ______________________ ______

FRIENDS (socializing, sports) ______________________ ______

HOMEWORK/PLANNING ______________________ ______

ALONE (playing, reading, thinking) ______________________ ______

CHORES/HOUSEWORK ______________________ ______

FAMILY (including shared mealtimes)______________________ ______

MISCELLANEOUS ______________________________ ______

If you had a terminal illness with six months to live,
how would you spend each twenty-four hours?

SLEEP ______________________________ ______
SCHOOL/MEETINGS ______________________________ ______
WORK (earning money) ______________________________ ______
FRIENDS (socializing, sports) ______________________________ ______
HOMEWORK/PLANNING ______________________________ ______
ALONE (playing, reading, thinking) ______________________________ ______
CHORES/HOUSEWORK ______________________________ ______
FAMILY (including shared mealtimes) ______________________________ ______
MISCELLANEOUS ______________________________ ______

How well do your priorities match up with the way you currently spend your time? How would you like to change this?

____

____

____

✦

Task F—Scheduling

1. On a separate sheet of paper, turned lengthwise, mark off seven columns and label each with a day of the week from Sunday to Saturday. In each column write times beginning from when you wake until when you typically go to sleep. Then write in what you do during each hour. Be sure to include time for driving from one place to another if that is relevant.

When you are done, look this over. How much time do you have for solitude? How much time do you spend with loved ones? How many of these tasks do you have a choice about? Have you made the right choices with your discretionary time? Write your comments below:

2. In order to have time for the reflection needed during a deep change like the one you are currently trying to make, you need plenty of time for thinking, journal writing, and constant reassessment. You should strive for one or two hours a day or ten hours a week of solitude. (If this seems impossible, consider how many hours a week you spent on your addiction in the past. Include hangover downtime.)

What activities or obligations can you omit so that you have more time for solitude and the things you consider most important?

3. What tasks can you delegate to others at work, or those in your home? Which can you let go undone?

Make another schedule that better reflects your needs and priorities at this time. Begin implementing it at once by cutting out all unnecessary obligations. Post it on your wall.

✦

Task G—Relaxation Suggestion

Sitting on a bar stool or tuning out with drugs is the antithesis of physical activity. You may not be ready to join a health club, but you may be able to get yourself moving by playing childhood games like Spud, Hide n' Seek, Kick the Can, Red Light/Green Light, Croquet, Badminton, Volley Ball, or Softball. There are also many non-competitive games that are pure joy for kids or adults. Check your library for these games and suggest them as a mixer for the office picnic, family party, or an afternoon cookout with friends. They are a great way of helping adults and children have fun together. If you feel too shy to lead the games, enlist a co-leader, assuring her that you will research the games if she will just give the directions when the time comes. Physical activity relieves tension and releases endorphins that lift depression. Your complete recovery will ultimately require you to include some form of exercise in your weekly plan. Games can add that extra spark of motivation.

✦

SEARCH FOR MEANING

Task H—More Questions

1. What would you wish for if you were granted three wishes?

____

____

____

2. What do you think you can do to leave the world a better place than you found it?

____

____

3. Do you believe that how you live your life will make any difference after you die? How and why or why not?

____

____

____

4. ACTION STEP: Make a difference.

We sometimes do not realize how even the smallest gesture on our parts can make a difference in someone's life, in a group's goal, or in a community's welfare. Some people prefer to work on a personal scale; some like to use their humble skills in bitsized pieces; still others prefer to act in the political realm. Decide on a "good deed" to do and commit yourself to taking the first step this week. I've provided some examples below.

Personal: Befriend a neighborhood child who looks like he or she needs attention; offer to shop for or visit an elderly shut-in; invite a lonely co-worker over for dinner.

Offering skills: Volunteer to type the minutes for your group; stuff envelopes for a mailing; plant flowers in a nearby park; offer to paint or make repairs on a community building.

Political gestures: Work up a petition that would initiate correction of a disturbing community problem; attend an open forum and stand up to give your views; write letters to your senators and representitives about an issue you feel is important.

Commitment: ____________________________________

____

✦

Part III: On-Going Step Work

For the categories listed below, please refer to the explanations given in the introduction.

✦ 1. **Stories of others that have helped me see myself.** Do you know anyone who would serve as a role model for deep and lasting changes? Is there anyone you would wish to become more like?

✦ 1. Stories of others that have helped me see myself. *(Continued)*

✦ 2. Relevant dreams.

✦ 2. Relevant dreams. *(Continued)*

✦ 3. Confessions.

✦ 3. Confessions. *(Continued)*

✦ 4. Small Progresses and Stepping Stones. (Brief descriptions.)

✦ 5. Conflicts and their resolution or non-resolution.

✦ 5. Conflicts and their resolution or non-resolution. *(Continued)*

✦ 5. Conflicts and their resolution or non-resolution. *(Continued)*

✦ 6. Reflections. (Date each entry)

✦ 6. Reflections. *(Continued)*

✦ 6. Reflections. *(Continued)*

✦ 6. Reflections. *(Continued)*

✦ 6. Reflections. *(Continued)*

STEP 8

Made a list of all persons we have harmed, became willing to make amends to them all, and to forgive those against whom we have held grudges.

Part I: The Meaning of Step 8[1]

It is part of our denial system to tell ourselves that we were the *only* ones hurt by our addiction and resulting behavior. Indeed, it is important not to overlook the injury we have caused ourselves. We may even want to put ourselves at the top of the list. But we are only rationalizing if we think that we are also the end of the list. We have hurt others in a million ways, some very subtle, some very obvious.

We have hurt our workplace, our boss, our customers, and our co-workers. Sure, we might have managed to keep our job, but what percentage of ourselves did we give to the job while we were drinking? When we came in with a hangover, were we really giving it our all? At a minimum, we have deprived them of our best effort.

Similarly, we have deprived our loved ones of our best attention. We may have caused them physical, mental, emotional, and spiritual damage. Our angry outbursts, deceptions, and sexual transgressions produce obvious harm to others close to us, but we must also be ready

1. You may wish to read Sidney B. Simon and Suzanne Simon, *Forgiveness: How to Make Peace With Your Past and Get on with Your Life* (New York: Warner Books, 1990) and Augustus Y. Napier with Carl Whitaker, *The Family Crucible* (New York: HarperPerennial, 1978).

to perceive and admit to our subtler harms. Our daily emotional tone may have been harmful to all those who had to work or live with us.

If we have been miserly, irresponsible, irritable, bitter, critical, or impatient, we have created daily stress and demoralization in others' lives and deep psychological damage in those very close to us. Children have few defenses against the callousness of addicted adults, and spouses hurt for both themselves and the children.

Worse than the time we failed to spend with them, the blame we may have heaped upon them (to try and escape our own feelings of guilt and shame) may have hurt them deeply. Our resentment tells them they are nothing but a chore; our intolerance tells them there is something wrong with them; our self-pity tells them they are the selfish ones; our self-righteousness tells them they are all wrong; and our lies cover up the rest of our faults, leaving them holding the bag, wondering why they were permitted to be born. Even on our better days, we often harmed them by neglect or inaction.

Through the self-centeredness that addiction causes, we may have also unwittingly done harm in the name of "helping" our family members. We may have pointed out their faults for them, or ignored who they are as individuals and pushed them in whatever direction served us best. By failing to do our share of the work, we created more work for others. Indeed, our shenanigans may have made us a heavy burden for them to carry on top of the normal day to day tasks.

We owe more than perfunctory apologies. For our remorse to sound sincere, and in order for others to be able to forgive us, we must state the specifics of our harmful behavior. If we cannot name the particular harms we have committed, others will fear that we will repeat them. We must show that we now know the difference between right and wrong, and that we now see our loved ones' vulnerabilities and are being careful to treat them with respect. Along with our apology for past transgressions we need to pledge reform. We need to be ready to say with confidence that we will do our best to avoid hurting them again in the future. If we have made apologies and promises in the past that we later broke, we cannot expect instant trust. We will have to prove our word over time by keeping our promises. If we have let our loved ones down for five years, we must be ready for them to take five years to trust us again.

We will know we are ready and *willing* for this step when we can apologize to those who have hurt us, when we don't follow the philosophy of "an eye for an eye" and cross off the list those who have gotten revenge or those whom we feel "deserved" our ill treatment. This step is not about judging others. We need to pull back into our humility and learn to replace judgment with attitudes of mercy and forgiveness. Whether our "enemies" ask for it or not, it is our responsibility to forgive them in our hearts and then apologize for our wrongdoing. This is the only attitude that will lead to emotional resolution.

We need to demonstrate a spirit of good will. In this spirit, we assume that no one has harmed us on purpose, that any pain inflicted on us was an accident of circumstance. We give them the benefit of the doubt. It is not our job or our concern to mention their transgressions or faults.

Don't forget to make amends to those from whom you have borrowed money or to whom you owe money. Instead of empty apologies, make payments on your debts. If you haven't paid child support in years, pledge to make it up. It is not only your moral duty, it is a statement to your children that you do consider them to be important. Forget your feelings toward your ex-spouse. Learn to keep your focus on what is intrinsically most important.

Some apologies will be easy. There will be acquaintances who were inconvenienced or insulted by you. Co-workers you have undermined or customers you have cheated will be much more difficult. You may cringe at the thought of actually admitting to your spouse or your children the many ways you have neglected or abused them. There may be shameful things you must confess. Since the list will be long, you should probably prepare it in writing. You may find it easier to send it in this form first, but you must let them know that you are willing to talk about it face to face when they are ready. This is the only kind of apology that can heal a deep wound.

Give them the opportunity to add other "crimes" to the list that you may have forgotten. Don't argue. Just apologize. Plan to sit it out and talk about the past until they feel like they can let it go.

The most difficult apologies will be those you must make to people you believe have harmed you even more than you harmed them. Your pride says that they should come apologize to you. Regardless of what other people may have done to you, you are responsible for your own actions. Even if you have only injured them in response to their attacks, you must acknowledge to yourself that you kept the conflict alive and probably even escalated it. Two wrongs don't make a right. You need to make amends for what you have done, without any expectation that they should apologize in return. Remember, hate hurts the hater more than the hated. In order to heal, you must forgive.

But keep in mind that forgiveness means truly letting go. Just excusing them for their transgression is not enough. You must give up all resentment.

✦

Part II: Workbook Section on Step 8

Task A—Injury to Self

Consider how you hurt yourself while practicing your addiction. Did you destroy important relationships? Lose good jobs? Humiliate yourself?

____

____

____

____

✦

Task B—Lost Time

How has the loss of your time spent in bars or recovering from hangovers injured yourself or others?

____

____

____

____

✦

Task C—The Quick List

Below you will make a complete list of everyone you have injured. Don't worry about who might be harmed by an apology; that's the next step. Here you fearlessly declare your guilt. Begin with your immediate family: spouse, children, parents, siblings. Then do your co-workers. Next march back through time in your mind, year by year, and record the wrongs that still haunt you.

Person	My Wrongdoing	Effect on Them	Effect on Me

(Continue on a separate sheet if necessary)

✦

Task D—Action Plan

Divide the above list of your wronged ones into the three categories below. Plan to apologize to the relatively easy ones first (small crimes, distant relations), then move to the difficult ones whom you have injured deeply (and those whom you hate!). Finally, record the people you are uncertain about. By the time you finish apologizing to the first two groups and have listened to their feedback, you will know whether or not you need to apologize to the people in the last column.

Easy	Difficult	Questionable

✦

BREATHER!

Task E—Peak Experiences

Somewhere, back there, before your addiction took over your life, you experienced moments of joy and accomplishment. As you look back on your life, what were the peak experiences you've nearly forgotten? A trip to the beach? A great achievement? Young love? Warm moments with a best friend? Have you ever felt so happy you wouldn't mind dying right then? Write about it below.

✦

Task F—Fears

What consequences do you fear in making your amends? What is the worst thing that can happen? What is the best thing that can happen? What is likely to happen?

FEARS ______________________________

____

WORST ______________________________

____

BEST ______________________________

____

PROBABLE ______________________________

____

✦

Task G—Forgiving

There will be many people we have wronged who have also wronged us. In order to be able to make our amends in a sincere and calm manner, we must first deal with our negative feelings toward them. If we do not forgive them before we approach them, we are likely to provoke an angry confrontation.

Get your anger out of your system first. Look for your own part in the conflict. Write until you are spent. Then put it away for a week and see if your emotions have cooled off a little. When you can feel calm, burn up the paper and leave the past behind.

List the letters of anger you feel you need to write here. Then write out each one on a separate piece of paper so you can destroy them when you are done.

___

___

___

___

___

___

___

___

___

✦

Task H—Relaxation Suggestion

The addicted have often wished away their bodies. Being drunk or stoned happens in the head and only the limitiations of our bodies, against enduring this punishment, stops us from going "higher." We pass out, we come down, we drop from exhaustion, or get paralyzingly ill.

In recovery, we need to reunite with our bodies. We need to find pleasure and reward in the physical. Sometimes we are too stuck to take charge of moving our bodies until we feel the reward of effort increasing strength. We must receive our pleasure passively.

One good way to begin this change is through massage. We can pay a masseuse or massage therapist, we can have massage exchanges with friends, or we can purchase massage appliances that help us work the knots out of our muscles with a minimum physical effort. Whirlpool baths, saunas, and hot tubs also introduce pleasant physical responses with little effort on our part.

As we begin to feel ready to be more active, Yoga is a good way to slide into more self-activated movement. Tai Chi is also a soothing slow-motion physical activity. We can often find TV shows or video tapes that teach these routines, and health clubs, YMCAs, or YWCAs may have steam rooms, saunas, or whirlpools. Check your local resources and plan to include soothing body sensations in this month's relaxation activities.

✦

SEARCH FOR MEANING

Task I—Changes

Many things affect us in long-lasting ways. People change us, ideas change us, books change us, world events change us, and personal life events such as parenting, the death of a loved one, or a serious illness change us. We can also make changes simply by deciding to do so, or resist destructive changes that seem to be forcing themselves on us. What major changes have you gone through in your life and what has caused or influenced those changes?

___

___

___

___

___

✦

Part III:
On-Going Step Work

For the categories listed below, please refer to the explanations given in the introduction.

✦ 1. Stories of others that have helped me see myself.

Has anyone ever surprised you by being the first to apologize for a fight you provoked?

✦ 1. Stories of others that have helped me see myself. *(Continued)*

✦ 2. Relevant dreams.

✦ 2. Relevant dreams. *(Continued)*

✦ 3. Confessions.

✦ 3. Confessions. *(Continued)*

✦ 4. Small Achievements and Stepping Stones. What is your apology history? Do you have any positive experiences with amends that you can draw on now?

✦ 5. Conflicts and their resolution or non-resolution.

Are there any long-standing conflicts you need to resolve? Is there anyone to whom you are no longer "speaking?"

✦ 5. Conflicts and their resolution or non-resolution. *(Continued)*

✦ 5. Conflicts and their resolution or non-resolution. *(Continued)*

✦ 6. Reflections. (Date each entry)

✦ 6. Reflections. *(Continued)*

✦ 6. Reflections. *(Continued)*

✦ 6. Reflections. *(Continued)*

✦ 6. Reflections. *(Continued)*

STEP 9

We made direct amends to such people wherever possible, except when to do so would injure them or others.

Part I: The Meaning of Step 9[1]

Our goal in Step 9 is to right whatever wrongs we have committed. In most cases this will lead to improved relationships with the injured parties. We will do our utmost to heal the wound, but if the other people cannot forgive us, we will accept that and not bother them with further contact. Once we have sincerely apologized, our part is done.

We need to have the proper attitude as we approach this step. First, it is good to have forgiven both ourselves and the people we injured, regardless of anything they might have done to retaliate. We will not succeed in resolving the conflict if we are still angry and defensive.

Second, we need to have a good idea going into the encounter about what we want to say and accomplish. Most importantly we want to make sure we state our apology without assigning any blame to the ones we injured. We must act responsibly as we make our confession and attempt amends, having thought through all the possible

1. You may wish to read William Ury, *Getting Past No: Negotiating with Difficult People* (New York: Bantam, 1991).

consequences so that we will not be caught off guard and be provoked to anger. A rehearsal with a sponsor, therapist, or friend may help prepare us.

We need to be open to any response we get from people we've injured, and be ready to accept their response without becoming angry. We are not there to manipulate them into forgiving us. In order to have this come off smoothly, we should make every effort to purge our bad feelings toward the person or incident before we meet to speak. This will help us resist the temptation to point out to them what we felt they did to provoke us. We are only there to talk about our own behavior.

It is also a good idea not to take the other person by surprise. They have a right to know that you intend to make amends. They have a right to refuse to let you do this at this time. They may feel too angry at you to face you just now. They may have some reason from the past to be frightened of you, or they may simply feel that they cannot handle seeing you right now, regardless of how you intend to behave. You can leave an open invitation to talk whenever and wherever they might feel comfortable at some time in the future.

It is best to think through all the possible consequences and responses to our confessions, so that we are not caught off guard. Most of the time the other person's response will be forgiving or tactful. We are starting on good ground at this point in our program. We should have been sober for several months by now so our head is clear and our reputation on the mend. Because we have demonstrated a very positive change, our injured friends will have more reason to believe us when we say that we will earnestly try to never hurt them like that again.

However, we must also be ready for some cold receptions. When we find ourselves in this situation, we want to be careful not to escalate the conflict by being defensive. When we feel defensive we are likely to act insulted or superior, pick at the other person's faults, start blaming others, or rationalizing our own irrational behaviors, and raise our voices or make threatening gestures. This not only does not accomplish what we wanted, it adds new abuse of the person to the list of past injuries!

There is actually a high probability that the injured person will initially make some accusations, complaints, or criticisms before they sense our sincerity. So how can we avoid blowing up at this point? By being prepared for negative responses, we can control our tempers better. We can be ready to actively listen to their comments and acknowledge that we have heard them by repeating the main ideas. It may be wise to avoid any response to these criticisms at this time. We can accomplish this without provoking them by simply thanking them for their honesty.

Try to avoid any confessions that would injure others. This is often a judgment call. We must be honest with ourselves about whether our attempt at amends will truly injure another or whether we are just using this possibility as an excuse to avoid a painful confrontation. Reasons not to make amends include not revealing an old affair to someone who had no idea it was going on if this will just hurt him or her unnecessarily, making a confession that would cause us to lose our jobs when someone is depending on our income, or forcing another who would like to avoid all contact with us to hear a confession we want to get off our chests.

As we begin this step we will want to use our best judgment, summon our courage, and pay attention to our timing. We don't want to approach the person until we are prepared to be calm. We want to be careful about the place where we make our confession and be sure that we will not embarrass the injured person. We probably don't want to discuss these highly personal issues in front of other people. If there is likely to be a strong emotional response, like crying, it is better not to meet in a very public place. On the other hand, if we have ever physically harmed the person, we should not suggest that we come to their home where they might feel trapped and vulnerable.

It is important to tell them exactly what we believe we did that harmed them, then ask how it was for them, seeking their viewpoint and feelings so they feel truly understood. Without defending ourselves or offering excuses or arguments, we can assure them that we will behave better in the future.

But what if the person has died or has moved away? In either case we can write a letter. For deceased friends, we can read the letter aloud at their grave site or some other place that reminds us of them. We can make our amends by donating to their favorite charity or by helping a close relative. If friends have moved away and have left an address, we can send a letter of apology and offer to accept a collect call if they would like to discuss the subject further.

It is never too late to make amends, and it is essential to our long-term sobriety to completely resolve issues that make us feel guilt and shame.

✦

Part II: Workbook Section on Step 9

Task A—Rehearsal

Write out each apology in full and read it to a sponsor or friend. Ask them to tell you if it feels like an attack, a defense, or is likely to "push the buttons" of the person you're trying to appease. Then role-play the actual meeting with your friend. You might like to try playing the part of your injured party.

Record here what you learned from your practice sessions:

____

____

____

____

____

✦

Task B—First Effort

How did your first apology go? What were you relieved about? What was hard to take? What did you learn about yourself from this? What will you do differently next time?

____

____

____

____

____

✦

Task C—Impressions

After you have done five apologies, record your impressions here. What are common reactions or themes? What has surprised you? What has disappointed you? How has this affected your total emotional state?

✦

Task D—Procrastination

Which apologies do you find yourself continuously putting off? What do you need to happen in order to feel like it is the right time to do them?

✦

Task E—Making Amends

How has making amends improved your relationships with others?

✦

Task F—Second Visits

Record here the names of people you feel need a second visit. What is your unfinished business? Is the person receptive to seeing you? What are your motives?

Name **Unfinished Business**

______ ______________________

______ ______________________

______ ______________________

✦

Task G—Themes

When you invited others to tell you how you had wronged them, what themes emerged? What emotions did you feel? How did you deal with your urge to defend yourself? Did you discover more amends you had to make?

____

____

____

____

✦

Breather!

Task H—Celebrate!

Plan a celebration for when you have finished making amends. Let it be a true celebration of your new life. Pay close attention to what you choose for beverages, food, and entertainment.

Who would you like to invite?

_______________ _______________

_______________ _______________

_______________ _______________

_______________ _______________

_______________ _______________

What day of the week will you have it? Choose an actual date.

____

What will you do for entertainment?

____

What will you do for food? (Consider lowering your anxiety by making it a potluck—low fat?)

____

____

____

What beverages will you serve?

_______________ _______________

_______________ _______________

Decorations or theme?

____

____

✦

Task I—Relaxation Suggestion

Remember summer days whiled away playing Candyland, Parchesi, Sorry!, Clue, or Monopoly? Traditional board games cost no more than two tickets to the movies. Revive an interest in Dominoes or Perquacky. Stay home and play board games with family or friends or organize a potluck party with a board game tournament. Order in pizza, fix fancy blender drinks with fruit, juice, and a little frozen yogurt. Or if you find yourself all alone, fix yourself a blender drink and put together a jigsaw puzzle. Play your nature sounds CD and pretend you are at the beach or shut in for a rainy day. Take the attitude that what you are supposed to be doing right now is enjoying yourself!

✦

THE SEARCH FOR MEANING

Task J—What Do You Worship?

We all worship something. We may not have planned rituals, but the way we live our lives shows what we worship. Some of us worship sports, others money, many in the United States worship material things. Some of us have also worshipped alcohol or TV. We might worship our jobs, our children, or our spouses. Some worship authority, change, truth, life, love, or sex.

What have you worshipped in the past, and what do you worship now? Is this something you would like to change about yourself? Why or why not?

Past worship ____

____

Present worship ____

____

Plan for future worship ___________________________________

____

✦

Part III: On-Going Step Work

For the categories listed below, please refer to the explanations given in the introduction.

✦ 1. Stories of others that have helped me see myself.

✦ 1. Stories of others that have helped me see myself. *(Continued)*

✦ 2. Relevant dreams.

✦ 2. Relevant dreams. *(Continued)*

✦ 3. Confessions.

✦ 3. Confessions. *(Continued)*

✦ 4. Small progresses and Stepping Stones (Brief descriptions.)

✦ 5. Conflicts and their resolution or non-resolution.

✦ 5. Conflicts and their resolution or non-resolution. *(Continued)*

✦ 5. Conflicts and their resolution or non-resolution. *(Continued)*

✦ 6. Reflections. (Date each entry)

✦ 6. Reflections. *(Continued)*

✦ 6. Reflections. *(Continued)*

✦ 6. Reflections. *(Continued)*

✦ 6. Reflections. *(Continued)*

STEP 10

Continued to take personal inventory and when we were wrong, promptly admitted it.

Part I: The Meaning of Step 10[1]

If we have conscientiously worked the program up to this point we may have already started reaping benefits. We have healed many troubled relationships, learned that it is okay to be our genuine selves, and are becoming free of guilt. But life goes on, and we will continue to make mistakes and have problems, just like everyone else in the universe. What will be different from this day forward, if we follow Step 10, is that we will deal with our problems while they are still small and manageable.

Living one day at a time not only means not worrying about the future, it also means not carrying yesterday's resentments or guilt into today. Through exercising Step 10, we can start with a clean slate every morning. In this way we can keep our lives free of guilt and other oppressive feelings that trigger relapse.

The first nine steps helped us establish new behavior patterns that will keep our lives sane. We must continue to be vigilant about spotting pride, fear, anger, self-pity, greed, selfishness, resentment, and dishonesty. We will continue to have these feelings, but now that our minds are clearer we will be able to spot them promptly and make corrections, apologies, and amends.

---

1. You may wish to read David D. Burns, *Feeling Good: The New Mood Therapy* (New York: NAL-Signet, 1980).

Some people are able to do this mentally, thinking through the day at bedtime. Some can even recognize these negative attitudes in the midst of their happening and immediately change gears. But most who have just reached Step 10 have to set aside thirty minutes a day to write and reflect. There are many ways to take a daily inventory.

We can keep a calendar for quick checks in which we rate our day on a scale of 1 to 10. When we realize we've had a bad day we can run our day past our internal "movie screen" until we recognize what is disturbing us. Some prefer to call a sponsor or friend to talk over each day because they feel safer having an objective person as a sounding board. Another method is to make a daily chart by drawing a line up the middle and dividing the paper into two columns: one for the successes of the day, and one for the errors. Whichever method we use, we should always remember to count our blessings as part of our inventory.

When we are more experienced, we will be able to master the "spot check." We can mentally "stop the action" in any uncomfortable situation and check our feelings and motives before we dig ourselves in any deeper. Another method of taking inventory is to take a long view. On each birthday or anniversary of sobriety, we can look back over the previous year and see how we have changed, calling to mind each of our recurring defects to see how much progress we have made in eliminating them.

Step 10 also tells us that when we are wrong, we should promptly admit it. First, especially if we are co-dependent, we want to be certain that we were in the wrong and not take on the blame for every problem around us. If we are at fault, we want to catch it as quickly as possible. In time, many Twelve Steppers learn to catch themselves right in the process of slipping. Perhaps they hear the belligerent tone of voice they are using or realize that they are becoming defensive. They stop themselves right there and make amends.

But it will take awhile for most of us to become that self aware. Daily written inventories are a crucial stepping stone to our journey of growing awareness. As we evaluate our days, we must stay focused on our own responsibility, our own reactions, and our own feelings. When we have wronged someone, even if we were relatively unaware of it at the time, we often carry an emotional hangover, a residue of guilt. If we are feeling tense or down at the end of the day, this may be a warning that we have unfinished business to sort out.

We can think over our encounters with other people that day and see if we can discover what we have done to make us feel guilty. Did we lose our tempers? Say something tactless? Arbitrarily refuse to cooperate with someone? Help spread gossip? Whatever we have done we can write about it in our journals and try to understand what triggered our inappropriate reactions. Then we can rewrite or visualize the scene with us doing the right thing so that when we face this situation again, we will have an alternative way of behaving. To wrap this up we need to think through how we will make amends the next day.

This is a life-long, never-ending task because we will never be perfect. And life is a continuing challenge because everything and everyone around us changes constantly. As soon as we learn how to deal with our child effectively, he enters a new stage with all new behaviors. As soon as we have total harmony with our neighbors, someone moves out and someone we don't understand moves in. As soon as we have learned to get along with everyone at work, we are given a cantankerous new boss.

Before each new shake-up, there is often a peaceful pause. We reach plateaus where we have corrected most of the destructive behaviors we were aware of and have not yet become aware of our other faults that need work. We can feel like a million dollars at these times, and we need to stop and relish the progress we have made. But this stage is as dangerous as it is wonderful.

When things are going great we are most vulnerable to falling back into our old addictions. Our lives may be going so well that we start to think we never really had a very serious problem, or that now we are so strong we could probably handle a drink or two. We may think we don't need meetings or sponsors anymore. And we slip.

When we feel ourselves losing the humility that has kept us sober, it is good to take a look back in our journals and read how life was as we were pulling ourselves out of our emotional trenches. We might also take a look at our unhealthy behaviors and see if any of them are starting to take root again. We want to discover them while they are small and pull them out like unwanted weeds. It is good to tell someone else about these discoveries because the act of speaking about them aloud helps fix them in our memories so that it will be harder to overlook them in the future.

If we genuinely feel that we are making little progress and are having extreme difficulty changing, it may be wise to see a therapist. Sometimes our self-tricks are too clever for a sponsor to handle and we need a professional to spot the ways we undermine our own progress. We may have brought so much baggage with us from our pasts that we need someone who can really push and probe while being supportive. We should have cleared most of this up by Step 10, and if we haven't, it's time to get help.

✦

Part II: Workbook Section on Step 10

Task A—Daily check-ups

1. Whom did I see today? What were my feelings during and after our encounter(s)?

Person	**Feelings During**	**Feelings Now**
__________	__________	__________
__________	__________	__________
__________	__________	__________

Do I have any amends to make? ____________________

What is my plan?

____

2. Assessment of my day:

Positives	**Negatives**
__________	__________
__________	__________
__________	__________
__________	__________
__________	__________

3. On a monthly calendar assess your day on a scale of 1 to 10, with 1 representing a very depressing or high conflict day and 10 representing a harmonious day of total peace. Do this every day for a month and at the end of the month look to see if there are any patterns connected to stress, menstrual cycles, encounters with certain people, lack of sleep, etc. Make a note of patterns you discover and indicate ways of dealing with them.

4. What is my plan to allow time for reflection each day?

____

____

✦

Task B—Weekly assessments

What new behaviors have I tried this past week?

____

____

What other behaviors would I like to try?

____

____

What is my plan for next week?

____

✦

BREATHER!

Task C—Strokes

What have I done this week that I am especially proud of? Describe it.

____

____

Did I catch myself in a "slip" of character and correct it right then? Describe it.

____

____

✦

Task D—Monthly assessment

1. In what ways is my life better now?

____

____

Have any problems grown worse?

____

2. Have I discovered any more defects since I did my Step 4 inventory? Have any old stubborn defects been impossible to shake?

____

____

3. Do I worry that I might need professional help? Where do I feel stuck?

____

____

✦

Task E—Relaxation Suggestions

Speed up your physical recovery by committing to some regular exercise at your own level. Start by strolling around the block or through the woods and gradually increase the challenge with hiking, brisk walking, or jogging. Get a neighbor or friend to pledge to join you at certain times, or get a dog. (They always love to walk and will encourage you to do so even when you're beat.) If you cannot find a pleasant environment or company to make the exercise more of a joy and less of a chore, try a Walkman radio or tape player and listen to music as you go. Experiment with different kinds of music to find the best one to fit your mood. I find Debussy soothing in the classical vein and Enya transports me with her New Age sound. Maybe you want to start by listening to slow music at your strolling stage and gradually increasing your fare to rock 'n roll to get your body moving faster. This kind of activity can release tensions at the end of the day (cocktail hour) or help you break the buildup of pressure at work by doing music and gentle exercise at lunchtime. Make a commitment to doing this regularly when you most need it, and design a reward for yourself when you keep that commitment.

✦

SEARCH FOR MEANING

Task F—Crises

The Chinese character for *crisis* is the combination of the characters for *danger* and *opportunity.* Some say that crises are "glorious opportunities fiendishly disguised as insoluble problems." Hidden in every painful problem is a stimulus to great new change. This optimistic, life-affirming view shows us that we can even feel grateful for terrible lows in our lives.

Now that you have worked through most of the steps, are you able to see positive value in your past mistakes?

What has your addiction added to your life, and how did this come about? What other painful difficulties have ultimately enriched your life?

____

____

____

____

____

✦

Part III:
On-Going Step Work

For the categories listed below, please refer to the explanations given in the introduction.

✦ 1. Stories of others that have helped me see myself.

✦ 1. Stories of others that have helped me see myself. *(Continued)*

✦ 2. Relevant dreams.

✦ 2. Relevant dreams. *(Continued)*

✦ 3. Confessions.

✦ 3. Confessions. *(Continued)*

✦ 4. Small progresses and Stepping Stones

✦ 5. Conflicts and their resolution or non-resolution.

✦ 5. Conflicts and their resolution or non-resolution. *(Continued)*

✦ 5. Conflicts and their resolution or non-resolution. *(Continued)*

✦ 6. Reflections. (Date each entry)

✦ 6. Reflections. *(Continued)*

✦ 6. Reflections. *(Continued)*

✦ 6. Reflections. *(Continued)*

✦ 6. Reflections. *(Continued)*

STEP 11

Through meditation and journaling we continually seek to clarify and improve our own judgment and to consider the best direction and purpose our lives can take.

Part I: The Meaning of Step 11[1]

In Step 10 we strove to be our best selves, learned to resolve conflicts as they arose, treated others the way we would wish to be treated, and learned to forgive ourselves for our occasional human foibles. As we continue these healthy attitudes and behaviors, we will be able to keep our lives steady on a day-to-day basis, but what of the larger picture? Do we have life goals we want to achieve? How do we accomplish the small steps that will ultimately lead to a sense of life well-spent? What is the best use of our talents and intelligence? We can't help wondering, "What is my destiny?"

We have now spent several months taking a painstakingly careful look at our strengths and weaknesses. How can we use our strengths and talents to ultimately leave the world a better place than it was when we arrived in it? How can we help preserve the quality of life for future generations?

---

1. You may wish to read M. Scott Peck, *The Road Less Traveled* (New York: Simon and Schuster, 1979). There is also a study guide meant to be used with small groups if you would like to start a discussion group. It is Alice Howard and Walden Howard, *Exploring the Road Less Traveled* (New York: Simon and Schuster, 1985). These are the essential guides to growing up for adult readers.

A life is made up of many small moments or decisions. We are often unconsciously driven in a certain direction that is not clear to us until much time has passed. When confronted with choices, how will we know which one will take us where we need to go? Sometimes an objective analysis will yield the answer, but often the final decision is based on a gut feeling we have about what is right for us. We take a risk and trust Providence that we have made the right decision.

By taking time each morning to listen to our still small voice within we can keep ourselves moving in the right direction. As long as we are governed by basic healthy human values we cannot go wrong. By now we have had many opportunities to sort and clarify—to learn to recognize our nobler impulses. By meditating or journal writing we can slow down sufficiently to recognize right from wrong, constructive from destructive, life-affirming from life-denying thoughts. We can begin to trust ourselves.

What do we stand for? What do we support? What is the philosophy or set of beliefs that guides our lives? We need to be aware of what we value most highly. If we do not try to bring these drives to consciousness, we can find ourselves headed in the wrong direction, lost at sea in a storm.

The Serenity Prayer offers a wise perspective:

> O, grant me the serenity,
> to accept the things I cannot change,
> courage to change the things I can,
> and wisdom to know the difference.

How do we gain that wisdom? Life experience is one good teacher. Unfortunately, while escaping into our addiction we could not benefit from life experience. In order to learn, we need to experience consequences of our actions, feel the pain of our mistakes, and sit through their aftermath. We avoided all this with our addiction. Many people in recovery feel like their emotional development came to a standstill when they began their addiction. They are now twenty-year-olds living in forty-year-old bodies. ACOAs may be even more immature because their parents were not role models of responsible adulthood. But our survival depends on making up this lost time as soon as possible.

In order to do this we need to pull every bit of knowledge out of our experiences from here on out. We must be constantly attentive to what life has to teach us. This means slowing down to absorb our experiences and reflecting on their meaning. We need to create quiet moments throughout the day when we can listen to our own better judgment rather than being pulled willy-nilly by the trends and opinions of the day.

Meditation, or taking time for reflection, is also effective for helping us notice what we have to be grateful for. As we count our blessings, we not only gain a more benevolent sense of life, we also learn what is truly important. We generally discover truths such as the fact that sharing moments with someone we love brings us deeper and more enduring satisfaction than material goods or worldly accomplishments. With such knowledge, we can gradually shape our lives so that we make the best of our days on earth.

All the world's religions have wisdom to share. Much of it overlaps or is simply restated in new ways. All seem to have a version of the golden rule: "Do unto others as you would have them do unto you." If we all earnestly tried to follow this one simple edict, there would be an end of war, famine, and just about every other evil on earth.

Wisdom is also found in the words of great thinkers and writers. Some of us are drawn to religious writings while others prefer to seek truth through philosophy or literature. Whatever medium we choose, we need to keep ourselves open and receptive.

We need a mind free of drugs, stimulants, or harmful influences and clear of intrusive or compulsive thoughts. We hear our inner voices best when our consciences are clear, our conflicts resolved, and we have peace of mind. For most, it takes at least two years of sobriety to be fully confident in our own best judgment. If you have been sober less time than that you might like to continue to use a therapist or wise friend as a sounding board before you make any big decisions, but try to think things through independently first so that you can see how trustworthy your own thought processes are at this point.

Some of us find we need a special environment to commune with our deepest thoughts. We might like to be at the ocean, in the forest, or on a mountaintop. Others can still their minds by taking an imaginary journey to such a place, a guided meditation. Some respond to carefully arranged holy places like churches, synagogues, mosques, or

Japanese gardens. Some must write to reach deep inside; some prefer to talk with like-minded friends. We each have our own best way of communicating with our core selves.

Step 11 demands that we not leave this to chance. We must actively plan to set aside the time we need to hear our inner thoughts. Otherwise we will find time passing and the "right moment" may never arrive.

Only by honoring our need to commune with our deepest selves and by conscientiously providing the time and opportunity to do so, can we learn to keep our lives in balance and harmony.

✦

Part II: Workbook Section on Step 11

Task A—Serendipity

Serendipity is happening upon some good luck when you were neither seeking nor expecting it. It is rather like grace. Has there ever been a time when a serendipitous coincidence helped clarify what direction your life should take? Describe the incident fully.

____

____

____

____

____

✦

Task B—Changing Direction

Can you recall a time when your life seemed to be headed in the wrong direction? What brought you back? Describe this fully including what you think you've learned from this experience.

____

____

____

____

____

✦

Task C—Beliefs

If a child asked you what you believe in, what would your answer be? Write the most complete answer you can.

✦

Task D—Wisdom

What are your favorite sources of wisdom or knowledge about healthy values? Has anything you've read or heard convinced you to change in some deep way? Explain in detail.

✦

Task E—Desert Island

If you were stranded on a desert island and one book floated to the shore, which book would you hope it would be? Why?

✦

Task F—One Week

If you had one week to live and unlimited resources, who would you gather around you and how would you pass the time? (Be creative! Assume that getting stoned or drunk no longer appeals to you.) Be thorough in your answer.

✦

Task G—Obituary

What would you like your obituary to say when you die? Write it out in complete form here.

____

____

____

____

____

✦

BREATHER!

Task H—Relaxation Suggestion

Reading is one of the oldest forms of relaxation. In school we have often been challenged to read texts that are dry or stretch us beyond our current reading level. When you read for relaxation it often helps to choose books that are below your best reading level. Children's picture books can be a delight as they stimulate pleasant visual responses, imagination, nostalgia, and ourselves as we were at a gentler, simpler time. Don't be embarrassed to bring ten home from the library even if you have no children (you can invent a nephew or niece for the librarian if you need to.)

Mysteries, romances, science fiction, and good literature can absorb our thoughts so thoroughly that we forget our problems and get ready for sleep. If you find reading to be "work" check out the books on tape at your library. These can even help you relax in a traffic jam. Or you might want to listen to recorded fairy tales as you soak in the tub. Don't listen to tapes or read books that "improve your mind" when you are trying to relax. Select pure fluff.

✦

THE SEARCH FOR MEANING

Task I—Plans

As you write towards the end of this journal, plan to keep the channel open between your conscious self and your inner voice. We have learned many methods to discover and strengthen that still small voice within, such as: 1) using a therapist or wise friend as a sounding board for our ideas, 2) making a habit of frequent reflection through journal writing or meditation, 3) risking new behaviors to test our growing knowledge about our needs and capabilities, and 4) forming the habit of reading materials that stimulate our deepest thoughts and teach us new ways of being. What are your plans for continuing to recognize that still small voice and facilitate its growth of wisdom? Be specific.

____

____

____

____

____

✦

Part III: On-Going Step Work

For the categories listed below, please refer to the explanations given in the introduction.

✦ 1. Stories of others that have helped me see myself.

✦ 1. Stories of others that have helped me see myself. *(Continued)*

✦ 2. Relevant dreams.

✦ 2. Relevant dreams. *(Continued)*

✦ 3. Confessions.

✦ 3. Confessions. *(Continued)*

✦ 4. Small Progresses and Stepping Stones

✦ 5. Conflicts and their resolution or non-resolution.

✦ 5. Conflicts and their resolution or non-resolution. *(Continued)*

✦ 5. Conflicts and their resolution or non-resolution. *(Continued)*

✦ 6. Reflections. (Date each entry)

✦ 6. Reflections. *(Continued)*

✦ 6. Reflections. *(Continued)*

✦ 6. Reflections. *(Continued)*

✦ 6. Reflections. *(Continued)*

STEP 12

Having developed deeper wisdom and an appreciation of the spiritual as a result of these steps, we tried to carry this message to other addicts and to practice these principles in all our affairs.

Part I: The Meaning of Step 12[1]

There are three important concepts in Step 12. First, that we have come to understand spiritual principles through our "Search for Meaning" exercises. We have learned that "spiritual" does not exclusively mean a belief in traditional concepts of God. Rather, spirituality is a way of approaching life. If we examine our own values and try to form a code of personal ethics that allows us to live in harmony with ourselves and others, we are living the spiritual life. Through the exercises in this book you have probably come to understand the importance of having and knowing good principles by which to live. You are in a far better position to determine what creates inspiration and hope in your life. This is "spirit."

Through personal growth and the overcoming of a tenacious, destructive habit, we have a new sense of confidence and well-being. We are once again capable of feeling joy as children do. Our lives have more meaning and purpose. We feel as if we have joined the flow of life, that transcendent feeling of being one with the universe. Life is no

1. If you have really enjoyed keeping a journal you are now ready to free-write in a blank journal book, or, if you like having structure and suggestions, you might like to try Ira Progoff, *At a Journal Workshop* (New York: Dialogue House Library, 1975).

longer something just to be endured; we look forward to each new day, whatever it brings. For we are learning to turn crises into opportunities. We can make good use of even the day's challenges and sorrows. This is spirit.

The second important point of Step 12 is that we will try to carry this message to others. Helping others in our 12 Step programs brings mutual benefits. The newcomer will be more likely to trust us because we have been through the mill ourselves. We also serve as living proof that abstinence can be achieved. On our end, we are reminded of the suffering caused by addiction, and seeing others at earlier stages fortifies our determination to remain sober. In addition, service to newcomers gives us a measure of our own progress toward recovery. Without this kind of contact, we are apt to get overconfident and consider becoming addicted again. (Five years sobriety is often a big danger point of overconfidence.)

The *Big Book* of Alcoholics Anonymous offers a lot of useful advice on the attitude we want to have to best capture the addict's attention and avoid alienating him or her. We are reminded of how defensive one feels in the beginning and warned against aggressive pushy tactics. This is where good grounding in conflict resolution skills can be a tremendous help. Newcomers are likely to be overcritical and resistant to new ideas. They must feel that each step they take is of their own choosing. Initially, we may be viewed with suspicion, and we need to keep our own defensive reactions in check.

The first goal is to establish rapport. We need to tell the newcomer enough about our own personal struggle to help her trust us and begin to feel a bond. In an unequal power situation such as this, in which you propose to help another almost as a teacher to a pupil, it is essential that the recipient not feel the obligation of charity—that uncomfortable feeling of receiving without giving anything in return. It helps the newcomer a great deal to know that she is helping you with your sobriety in return. Emphasize the benefits you derive from helping others in this way.

Avoid arguing or debating with the newcomer by emphasizing that each individual must decide what works best for himself. Make it clear that you realize that you can only say what has worked best for you and hope it offers the newcomer some useful insights.

Just be supportive. A hug, a phone call, or a greeting card can all be more powerful than we realize. By the time most addicts are seriously ready to change their habits, they have often alienated their friends and families. Small caring gestures can be profoundly uplifting for one who has hit bottom.

Finally, *Twelve Steps and Twelve Traditions* warns us to keep our humility while we help others. When we have a very responsive newcomer, there is a tremendous temptation to get a puffed up view of our own wisdom and power. We must remember that even though some of our suggestions were extremely effective and our newcomer seems eager for more, we do not know everything the newcomer needs to know. We must hold ourselves back from becoming too eager or directive.

As our newcomer gets stronger she will inevitably become more independent. This is a healthy thing. We need to know when to let go and let the newcomer rely more on herself. At the same time, we must detach enough to see that when a newcomer pulls back in strength, it is not a rejection of us. Just as parents often feel fulfilled and proud when their children no longer need them, Twelve Steppers can recognize their jobs are done when their newcomers can stand on their own.

The third goal of the Twelfth step—practicing the principles of the steps in all our affairs—actually presents the greatest challenge. It is no small order to try to live our values in all we do. This means resolving our conflicts at work, at home, among friends, and even with strangers. If we feel a clash, we are hereby pledging to make amends and clean the slate as soon as possible. Hopefully, we can even reach a level of self-awareness where we can see conflict coming and act swiftly enough to prevent it.

We can often keep our lives free of destructive conflict by focusing on the wisdom of this three-point pledge:

I will not pose enemies.
I will resolve conflict.
I will not use violence.[2]

---

2. Beyond War, Palo Alto, CA. This group offered conflict resolution training during the 1980s.

These principles can prevent conflicts or resolve conflicts before they escalate into full scale wars.

Our culture has encouraged competition or the habit of proving our worth in comparison to others. We jockey for position and fight to win arguments. The result is usually one winner and one loser. One leaves feeling victorious and superior, while the other is left feeling inadequate and resentful. Conflict resolution theory shows us that conflicts can be resolved cooperatively so that both depart feeling like winners in some sense. This leaves the door open for harmonious relations in the future.

How do the three basic conflict resolution principles help us accomplish this? First, if we refuse to think of our opponents as enemies, we will remain respectful of their need to be highly regarded. We refuse to put them down or trick them into accepting a solution that only benefits us. Just because our needs are in conflict with the needs of other's, we do not need to vilify or destroy them in order to get our way. That is how it has been done too long in our competitive society. Put-downs and tricks just leave our opponent feeling wronged and vengeful. By refusing to dehumanize our opponents by labeling them as the enemy, we begin our negotiations on more equal and respectful footing.

The second principle ("I will resolve conflict") reminds us that we cannot truly keep the peace by avoiding conflict because the problem will not just go away. An ignored conflict is like a festering wound that will eventually destroy the whole body if it is not taken care of.

Conflicts are not in and of themselves destructive. Almost all growth and exciting new ideas began with a conflict or problem. Conflict is the stimulus for change. Our own internal conflict with our addiction was the spark that caused us to adopt new ways through a Twelve Step program. So conflicts must be addressed in a constructive manner.

The third principle ("I will not use violence") points the way toward a constructive, effective solution. By violence we mean any action that will harm another. We all know how easy it is to heat up a conflict with verbal insults. We don't need to drop bombs to do long-lasting damage to a relationship. When we use any form of violence to get our way, our success will be short-lived. We can expect retaliation in the form of either counter-aggression or passive resistance. If we want true cooperation and an end to the conflict, we must consider the needs of our opponent and work toward a solution that leaves both parties feeling as if they have gained something.

By heeding these principles of nonviolent conflict resolution, we will find it easier to keep our Step 12 promise of bringing our newfound wisdom and harmony to bear on all areas of our lives.

✦

Part II: Workbook Section on Step 12

Task A—Review of the steps

The steps teach us about honesty, hope, faith, courage, humility, self-discipline, perseverance, and charity. In what ways has your grasp of these qualities improved since you began the program? In each category below, share a recent incident that you feel shows your growth in these areas:

HONESTY ______________________________

____

HOPE ______________________________

____

FAITH ______________________________

____

COURAGE ______________________________

____

HUMILITY ______________________________

____

SELF-DISCIPLINE ______________________________

____

PERSEVERANCE ______________________________

____

CHARITY ______________________________

____

✦

Task B—Greeting Newcomers

Have you been able to reach out to a newcomer yet? Describe below how you achieved this, or what you think you can offer a newcomer at this point.

____

____

____

✦

Task C—Reaching newcomers[3]

Which of the following techniques do you think would put a newcomer at ease? (Hint: There are eight good choices.)

1) Listen, then list your rebuttals; 2) Explore options; 3) Observe, reflect other's behavior objectively; 4) Assume you know what they mean; 5) Defend your position; 6) Listen, then list their points; 7) Give answers; 8) Give advice; 9) Share ideas and information; 10) Overcome objections; 11) Hear their position; 12) State what you hear, check it; 13) Interpret and judge other's behavior; 14) Ask "Why don't you?"; 15) Respect differences; 16) Ask "How can we?"

____

____

____

____

____

____

3. Answers to Task C, Task E, and Task F are given in an endnote to this chapter.

Task D—Testimonial

What would you say if someone asked you if the Twelve Step program has worked for you? Would you recommend it to others? Elaborate in detail.

Task E—Conflict resolution

How do you usually handle conflicts? Examine the list below and note how often you use each device by placing an X under Frequently (F), Occasionally (O), or Rarely (R). Then in front of each number put a letter from the following code: V for violent, N for not really effective, S for sometimes effective, and G for often effective. Then analyze your answers in the questions that follow.

	F	*O*	*R*
1. Avoid the person	___	___	___
2. Change the subject	___	___	___
3. Try to understand the other person's point of view	___	___	___
4. Try to turn the conflict into a joke	___	___	___
5. Admit that you are wrong even if you do not believe you are	___	___	___
6. Give in	___	___	___

7. Apologize ___ ___ ___
8. Try to find out specifically what you agree on and disagree on to narrow down the conflict ___ ___ ___
9. Try to reach a compromise ___ ___ ___
10. Pretend to agree ___ ___ ___
11. Get another person to decide who is right ___ ___ ___
12. Threaten the other person ___ ___ ___
13. Fight it out physically ___ ___ ___
14. Whine or complain until you get your way ___ ___ ___
15. Play the martyr, give in, but let the other person know how much you are suffering ___ ___ ___
16. Get revenge in a passive-aggressive manner ___ ___ ___

Are there any techniques above that you use often that are not really effective?

___

Are there any techniques above you rarely use that would be quite effective?

___

What has proven to be the most effective technique for you?

___

Choose one technique that you believe can be the best alternative in some situations but a poor choice in other situations. Explain why.

___

___

___

✦

Task F—Escalation of Conflict

Choose from the list below and decide which actions would escalate or de-escalate a conflict. Place your answer under the appropriate heading. (Hint: Eight of these will *escalate* the conflict.)

1) Insults/name calling; 2) Actively listen; 3) Raise voice; 4) Silent treatment;

5) Look for common ground; 6) Treat other person with respect; 7) Focus on the problem/not the person; 8) Blame other; 9) Compromise; 10) Set future time to resolve conflict; 11) Bring up the past; 12) Brainstorm for alternatives; 13) Interrupt other; 14) Good natured humor; 15) Change the subject; 16) Apologize if you are wrong; 17) State position clearly; 18) Shake your finger at other; 19) Keep voice tone calm.

Escalate	De-Escalate
________________	________________
________________	________________
________________	________________
________________	________________
________________	________________
________________	________________
________________	________________
________________	________________
	________________
	________________
	________________

✦

BREATHER!

Task G—Relaxation Suggestion

A good way to release our aggressive feelings is through vigorous physical exercise. A good sweat followed by a shower is perhaps the best way to release tension and help us get our world views and attitudes back in perspective. The artistically inclined may do best with folk dancing or aerobic dancing done to lively tunes, while the more athletic may prefer a workout at a health club that challenges their muscles with weight routines or Nordic tracks. Some do best with a disciplined schedule set up beforehand by signing up for a class or having an appointment with a trainer, while others need the flexibility one can only get by having equipment and exercise videos to follow at home. Most video stores rent out exercise tapes so you can experiment and see which ones best suit your needs.

Addiction is a slow form of suicide. Each day we are addicted, we accept that our lives will probbaly be shortened a little by our current activities. It is a giant step toward total recovery when we can focus on activities that may prolong our lives, or at least recoup some of the physical health we gave up before. It is a decision to live, to love life so much that you actually want as much of it as you can get. Grab some life for yourself and don't let go!

✦

Search for Meaning

Task H—Spiritual paths

> *Look at every path closely and deliberately. Try it as many times as you think necessary. Then ask yourself, and yourself alone, one question . . . Does this path have a heart? If it does, the path is good; if it doesn't it is of no use. Both paths lead nowhere; but one has a heart, the other doesn't.*
>
> from *The Teachings of Don Juan*
> by CARLOS CASTENADA

The central message of the Twelfth Step is the call to share your newfound emotional stability with someone who is yet struggling. It is generally the Twelve Step way to turn and help others who are just beginning their journey back to sanity. Certainly, these people need help and guidance from those more experienced.

But giving something back to the world need not be limited to Twelve Step programs. You may have other causes you believe in that you want to support. Perhaps you enjoy working with children or the elderly, or you are deeply concerned about the environment. The important thing is the effort of reaching out to help others in need.

We will not always be successful in "saving" those we seek to help. That is why we must keep our eye on the path. It may lead nowhere but we will have served the cause of making the world a better place just through our process of trying. We are bringing charity and hope to where there may have been none.

What paths feel like they have a "heart" for you? What can you give to keep your sobriety? List three possibilities here and commit to finding out more about them.

1. ______________________________

2. ______________________________

3. ______________________________

✦

Part III: On-Going Step Work

For the categories listed below, please refer to the explanations given in the introduction.

✦ 1. Stories of others that have helped me see myself.

✦ 1. Stories of others that have helped me see myself. *(Continued)*

✦ 2. Relevant dreams.

✦ 2. Relevant dreams. *(Continued)*

✦ 3. Confessions.

✦ 3. Confessions. *(Continued)*

✦ 4. Small Achievements and Stepping Stones.

✦ 5. Conflicts and their resolution or nonresolution.

✦ 5. Conflicts and their resolution or nonresolution. *(Continued)*

✦ 5. Conflicts and their resolution or nonresolution. *(Continued)*

✦ 6. Reflections. (Date each entry)

✦ 6. Reflections. *(Continued)*

✦ 6. Reflections. *(Continued)*

✦ 6. Reflections. *(Continued)*

✦ 6. Reflections. *(Continued)*

ANSWERS TO TASKS C, E, F.

Task C: Good techniques are 2, 3, 6, 9, 11, 12, 15, 16.

Task E: Though opinions sometimes vary on which of these is violent, effective or ineffective, here's what I think: 1.V,N 2.V,S 3.G 4.S 5.S 6.N 7.G 8.G 9.G 10.N 11.S 12.V,N 13.V 14.V 15.V 16. V

Task F: Those which escalate conflict are: 1, 3, 4, 8, 11, 13, 15, 18

Conclusion

The Road Not Taken

Two roads diverged in a yellow wood,
And sorry I could not travel both
And be one traveler, long I stood
And looked down one as far as I could
To where it bent in the undergrowth;

Then took the other, as just as fair,
And having perhaps the better claim,
Because it was grassy and wanted wear;
Though as for that the passing there
Had worn them really about the same,

And both that morning equally lay
In leaves no step had trodden black.
Oh, I kept the first for another day!
Yet knowing how way leads on to way,
I doubted if I should ever come back.

I shall be telling this with a sigh
Somewhere ages and ages hence;
Two roads diverged in a wood, and I—
I took the one less traveled by,
And that has made all the difference.

Robert Frost

Happiness lies not in getting what you want, but in wanting what you've got. We know we have healed and made full use of the pain and difficulties in our lives when we can see their value as learning experiences. Our descent into addiction and our struggle to come back have actually taught us a great deal about what we don't want. But that is a very valuable lesson.

So often people take what they have for granted, failing to notice the meaning, comfort, and richness that the simplest blessings can give us. We feel tormented because we don't have a better car or a bigger house as if these were the keys to happiness, foolishly ignoring the value of the family with whom we share our space.

A paraplegic is acutely aware of the freedom of movement he or she has lost—yet that freedom of movement is something the rest of us don't cherish properly. As the saying goes, "You don't know what you've got until you lose it."

Our addictions have caused many of us to lose it all. As we work towards sobriety and let go of denial, we are suddenly painfully aware of the value of what we have lost.

Robert Frost did not believe that going back was really possible "knowing how way leads on to way." His poem reminds us of the old adage: "You can never go home again." Most doubt that there can be a return to innocence once we have experienced the evils of the "real" world.

But I have known many who are more innocent and trusting at age 45 than they were at age 25. Cynicism is a common stage of adolescence as teens realize that parents, teachers, and other adults around them are not perfect. This disillusionment is aggravated and exaggerated if young adults get involved in an addictive life-style. Indeed, the adults with whom they surround themselves may repeatedly prove to be self-centered and unreliable, if not vicious and cruel. Those who get involved in addictions take up residence in the dark side of life.

When we choose to give up those addictions and pursue recovery, we are catapulted over the wall into a realm of greater health and optimism—a place where others are trying to be their better selves and treat each other gently. For those whose childhoods were spent in troubled families, this new land can spark feelings of trust and innocence they have never known before.

What Robert Frost didn't say is that we *can* go back and try that other trail, and at a later stage in life we can still learn much from that choice. If we'd begun with the other trail we might have been mildly, pleasantly aware of its beauty. But if we take that trail after having taken the harder one, when we walk down that path we will be wonderfully aware of the smell of the grass and honeysuckle, the sounds of birds singing and chattering, the feel of the soft rich earth beneath our feet, and the rays of the sun spiking through the leaves. We will know the value of peace because we have experienced the darkness and terror of alienation.

When you count your blessings, be sure to put your addiction on the list. Like one who comes back from a near-death experience, we vibrate with appreciation for the simple things in life. That is the greatest of blessings.

APPENDIX

The Twelve Steps for Diversity

STEP 1: We admitted we were powerless over our addiction/compulsion—that our lives had become unmanageable.

STEP 2: Came to believe that, like all human beings, our power was limited and we needed to learn to let go and learn from others.

STEP 3: Made a decision to let go of control, assume a spirit of goodwill, seek the wisdom of responsible others, and discover our true "voice within."

STEP 4: Made a searching and fearless inventory of our strengths and weaknesses.

STEP 5: Admitted to our journal, ourselves, and to another human being the exact nature of our wrongs.

STEP 6: Were entirely ready to listen to wise counsel and seek that still small voice within to guide us to change our behaviors which have been harmful to ourselves and others.

STEP 7: Humbly begin the process of deep change so we could overcome our weaknesses.

STEP 8: Made a list of all persons we have harmed, became willing to make amends to them all, and to forgive those against whom we have held grudges.

STEP 9: Made direct amends to such people wherever possible, except when to do so would injure them or others.

STEP 10: Continued to take personal inventory and when we were wrong, promptly admitted it.

STEP 11: Through meditation and journaling we continually seek to clarify and improve our own judgment and to consider the best direction and purpose our lives can take.

STEP 12: Having developed deeper wisdom and an appreciation of the spiritual as the results of these steps, we tried to carry this message to other addicts and to practice these principles in all our affairs.

The Twelve Steps of Alcoholics Anonymous

STEP 1: We admitted we were powerless over alcohol—that our lives had become unmanageable.

STEP 2: Came to believe that a power greater than ourselves could restore us to sanity.

STEP 3: Made a decision to turn our will and our lives over to the care of God as we understood Him.

STEP 4: Made a searching and fearless moral inventory of ourselves.

STEP 5: Admitted to God, to ourselves and to another human being the exact nature of our wrongs.

STEP 6: Were entirely ready to have God remove all these defects of character.

STEP 7: Humbly asked Him to remove our shortcomings.

STEP 8: Made a list of all persons we have harmed, and became willing to make amends to them all.

STEP 9: Made direct amends to such people wherever possible, except when to do so would injure them or others.

STEP 10: Continued to take personal inventory and when we were wrong, promptly admitted it.

STEP 11: Sought through prayer and meditation to improve our conscious contact with God as we understood Him, praying only for knowledge of His will for us and the power to carry that out.

STEP 12: Having had a spiritual awakening as the result of these steps, we tried to carry this message to other addicts, and to practice these principles in all our affairs.

The Twelve Steps: A Nontheistic Translation[1]

1. Admit we are powerless over other people, random events and our own persistent negative behaviors, and that when we forget this, our lives become unmanageable.

   Principles: Insight, Honesty

2. Came to believe that spiritual resources can provide power for our restoration and healing.

   Principles: Hope, Faith

3. Make a decision to be open to spiritual energy as we take deliberate action for change in our lives.

   Principles: Decision, Acceptance, Action

4. Search honestly and deeply within ourselves to know the exact nature of our actions, thoughts and emotions.

   Principles: Self-examination, Personal honesty, Self-acceptance

5. Will talk to another person about our exact nature.

   Principles: Trust, Personal integrity

6. Be entirely ready to acknowledge our abiding strength and release our personal shortcomings.

   Principle: Willingness to change

7. Work honestly, humbly and courageously to develop our assets and to release our personal shortcomings.

---

1. Martha Cleveland and Arlys G., *The Alternative 12 Steps: A Secular Guide to Recovery* (Deerfield Beach, FL: Health Communications, Inc., 1992).

Principles: Personal responsibility, Involvement in change, Courage, Humility, Self-discipline

8. List all people we have harmed, including ourselves, and be willing to make amends to them all. Be willing to forgive those who have harmed us.

Principles: Compassion, Personal honesty and Accountability

9. Whenever possible, we will carry out unconditional amends to those we have hurt, including ourselves, except when to do so would cause harm.

Principles: Compassion, Change, Honesty and Responsibility, Forgiveness, Self-Discipline

10. Continue to monitor ourselves, to acknowledge our successes and quickly correct our lapses and errors.

Principles: Perseverance, Integrity

11. Increasingly engage spiritual energy and awareness to continue to grow in abiding strength and wisdom and in the enjoyment of life.

Principles: Openness, Connection to life and spiritual resources

12. Practice the principles of these steps in all our affairs and carry the Twelve-Step message to others.

Principles: Commitment, Self-discipline, Service to others.

The Thirteen Statements of Women for Sobriety[2]

1. I have a drinking problem that once had me.
2. Negative emotions destroy only myself.
3. Happiness is a habit I will develop.
4. Problems bother me only to the degree I permit them to.
5. I am what I think.
6. Life can be ordinary or it can be great.
7. Love can change the course of my world.
8. The fundamental objective of life is emotional and spiritual growth.
9. The past is gone forever.
10. All love given returns.
11. Enthusiasm is my daily exercise.
12. I am a competent woman and have much to give others.
13. I am responsible for myself and my actions.

2. In Charlotte Davis Kasl, *Many Roads, One Journey: Moving Beyond the Twelve Steps* (New York: HarperPerennial, 1992), p. 167.

Sixteen Steps for Discovery and Empowerment[3]

1. We affirm we have the power to take charge of our lives and stop being dependent on substances or other people for our self-esteem and security.

2. We come to believe that God/the Goddess/Universe/Great Spirit/Higher Power awakens the healing wisdom within us when we open ourselves to that power.

3. We make a decision to become our authentic Selves and trust in the healing power of the truth.

4. We examine our beliefs, addictions, and dependent behavior in the context of living in a hierarchal, patriarchal culture.

5. We share with another person and the Universe all those things inside of us for which we feel shame and guilt.

6. We affirm and enjoy our strengths, talents, and creativity, striving not to hide these qualities to protect others' egos.

7. We become willing to let go of shame, guilt, and any behavior that keeps us from loving ourselves and others.

8. We make a list of people we have harmed and people who have harmed us, and take steps to clear out negative energy by making amends and sharing our grievances in a respectful way.

9. We express love and gratitude to others, and increasingly appreciate the wonder of life and the blessings we *do* have.

10. We continue to trust our reality and daily affirm that we see what we see, we know what we know, and we feel what we feel.

---

3. Charlotte Davis Kasl, *Many Roads, One Journey: Moving Beyond the Twelve Steps* (New York: HarperPerennial, 1992).

11. We promptly acknowledge our mistakes and make amends when appropriate, but we do not say we are sorry for things we have not done and we do not cover up, analyze, or take responsibility for the shortcomings of others.

12. We seek out situations, jobs, and people that affirm our intelligence, perceptions, and self-worth and avoid situations or people who are hurtful, harmful, or demeaning to us.

13. We take steps to heal our physical bodies, organize our lives, reduce stress, and have fun.

14. We seek to find our inward calling, and develop the will and wisdom to follow it.

15. We accept the ups and downs of life as natural events that can be used as lessons for our growth.

16. We grow in awareness that we are interrelated with all living things, and we contribute to restoring peace and balance on the planet.

The Twelve Steps of SOS[4]

1. I learned that I am not able to control __________ and that when I ignore this fact I make my life unmanageable.

2. I came to believe that, with the help and support of others in situations similar to mine, I could again find my sanity.

3. I made a decision to act on this belief, to stop trying to fix things myself, and to accept the concern and assistance available to me.

4. I began to make a searching and fearlessly honest inventory of myself.

5. I candidly acknowledged to myself, and to others in whom I chose to confide, exactly how my conduct in the past had brought me needless unhappiness.

6. I became entirely ready to change my behavior in ways that could bring me the quality of life I wanted.

7. I gradually put aside any denial, pretense and disdain, any pointless willfulness I may have had, and in choosing recovery I began once again to grow healthy.

8. I made a list of all persons I could remember who had been harmed by my past behavior and became willing to reach out to them all in conciliation.

9. I directly contacted each of these persons, genuinely expressed my regrets and apologies, and tried to restore harmony between us—except when in my judgment to do so would cause further harm to any of us.

10. I continue to take personal inventories, and when I find myself off

---

4. Although some SOSers want nothing to do with the Twelve Steps (usually because they bring back painful memories of coercion and alientation), this rendition did appear in the *Atlanta Journal*, February 5, 1990.

my chosen course, I try to admit it promptly and to make immediate correction.

11. I regularly take quiet times to increase my awareness of the many sources of strength available to me, being open to all that will enrich my life, and being willing always to learn.

12. Being more alert now as a result of living through these steps, I try to communicate these experiences to others. And I try daily to practice these principles in all my affairs.

The Six Guidelines of SOS

1. To break the cycle of denial and achieve sobriety, we first acknowledge that *we are alcoholics.*

2. We *reaffirm* this truth daily and accept without reservation—one day at a time—the fact that as sober alcoholics, we cannot and do not drink, *no matter what.*

3. Since drinking is not an option for us, we take whatever steps are necessary to continue our sobriety priority lifelong.

4. A high quality of life—the good life—can be achieved. However, life is also filled with uncertainties; therefore, we do not drink regardless of feelings, circumstances, or conflicts.

5. We share in confidence with each other our thoughts and feelings as sober alcoholics.

6. Sobriety is our priority and we are each individually responsible for our lives and our sobriety.

Bibliography

Books and Articles

Al-Anon Family Groups. (1981). *Al-Anon's Twelve Steps and Twelve Traditions*. New York.

Al-Anon Family Groups. (1992). *Courage to Change*. New York.

Al-Anon Family Groups. (1994). *From Survival to Recovery: Growing Up in an Alcoholic Home*. New York.

Al-Anon Family Groups. (1976). *Living With an Alcoholic*. New York.

Alcoholics Anonymous World Services, Inc. (1976). *Alcoholics Anonymous*. 3rd ed. New York.

Alcoholics Anonymous World Services, Inc. (1990). *Came to Believe*. New York.

Alcoholics Anonymous World Services, Inc. (1987). *Living Sober.* New York.

Alcoholic Anonymous World Services, Inc. (1993). *Twelve Steps and Twelve Traditions: An Interpretive Commentary on the A.A. Program*. New York.

Beacon Press Staff. (1989). *On The Path: Spirituality for Youth and Adults*. Boston: Beacon Press.

Beattie, Melody. (1987). *Codependent No More* New York: Harper-Collins.

Berman, Marvin. (1992). *Working Effectively With MICA Clients in Community Residences*. Philadelphia, PA: MICARE.

Bloomfield, Harold H., and Leonard Felder. (1983). *Making Peace with Your Parents*. New York: Ballantine Books.

Boraks, Lucius. (1988). *Religions of the East.* Kansas City, MO: Sheed and Ward.

———. (1988). *Religions of the West.* Kansas City, MO: Sheed and Ward.

Burns, David D. (1981). *Feeling Good: The New Mood Therapy.* New York: NAL-Signet.

Cermak, Timmen L., and Jacques Rutzky. (1994). *A Time To Heal Workbook.* New York: Putnam.

Chinen, Allan B. (1993) *Once Upon a Midlife.* New York: Putnam.

Christopher, James. (1988). *How to Stay Sober: Recovery without Religion.* Buffalo, NY: Prometheus Books.

———. (1992). *SOS Sobriety: The Proven Alternative to Twelve-Step Programs,* Buffalo, NY: Prometheus Books.

Cleveland, Martha, and Arlys G. Cleveland (1992). *The Alternative Twelve Steps: A Secular Guide to Recovery.* Deerfield Beach, FL: Health Communications.

Clinebell, Howard J. (1968). *Understanding and Counseling the Alcoholic.* Nashville, TN: Abingdon Press.

Cohen, Jacqueline, and Stephen Jay Levy. (1992). *The Mentally Ill Chemical Abuser: Whose Client?* New York: Lexington Books.

Custer, Robert, and Harry Milt. (1985). *When Luck Runs Out: Help for Compulsive Gamblers and Their Families.* New York: Facts on File Publications.

Dorsman, Jerry. (1994). *How to Quit Drinking Without AA: A Complete Self-Help Guide.* Rocklin, CA: Prima Publishing.

Evans, Katie, and J. Michael Sullivan. (1990). *Dual Diagnosis: Counseling the Mentally Ill Substance Abuser.* New York: Guilford Press.

Fassel, Diane. (1990). *Working Ourselves to Death: The High Cost of Workaholism and the Reward of Recovery.* San Francisco: Harper.

Fisher, Roger. *Elements of Negotiation.* (1987) Audiotape. New York: Caedmon Audio.

Fox, Vince. (1993). *Addiction, Change and Choice.* Tuscon, AZ: Sharp Press.

Gackenhach, Jayne, and Jane Bosveld. (1990). *Control Your Dreams.* New York: HarperPerennial.

Gamblers Anonymous. (1994). *Sharing Recovery through Gamblers Anonymous.* Los Angeles.

Gilbert, Richard S. (1983). *Building Your Own Theology.* Boston, MA: Unitarian Universalist Association.

Gold, Mark S., with Lois B. Morris (1988). *The Good News About Depression: Cures and Treatments in the New Age of Psychiatry.* New York: Bantam Books.

"Health Report." (30 January 1995). *Time.*

Howard, Alice, and Walden Howard. (1985). *Exporing the Road Less Travelled.* New York: Simon and Schuster.

Kasl, Charlotte Davis. (1992). *Many Roads, One Journey: Moving Beyond the Twelve Steps.* New York: HarperPerennial.

Keirsey, David, and Marilyn Bates. (1984). *Please Understand Me: Character and Temperament Types.* Del Mar, CA: Prometheus Nemesis Book Company.

Keen, Sam, and Anne Valley-Fox. (1989). *Your Mythic Journey.* Los Angeles: Jeremy P. Tarcher.

Kinder, Melvyn. (1994). *Mastering Your Moods.* New York: Simon and Schuster.

Kirkpatrick, Jean. (1990). *Turnabout: New Help for the Woman Alcoholic.* New York: Bantam.

Lerner, Harriet Goldhor. (1989). *The Dance of Intimacy.* New York: Harper and Row.

Looney, John. (1984). *Alternatives to Violence.* Akron, OH: Peace Grows.

Marshak, David, Ed. (1989). *On the Path: Spirituality for Youth and Adults.* Boston, MA: Unitarian Universalist Association.

"Moderation Management." (11 March 1995). *Newsweek.*

Napier, Augustus Y., and Carl Whitaker. (1988). *The Family Crucible.* New York: HarperCollins.

Narcotics Anonymous. (1987). *Narcotics Anonymous.* 4th ed. Van Nuys, CA.

Oliver-Diaz, Phillip, and Patricia O'Gorman. (1988). *Twelve Steps to Self-Parenting.* Deerfield Beach, FL: Health Communications.

Olitzky, Kerry M., and Stuart A. Copans. (1991). *Twelve Jewish Steps to Recovery.* Woodstock, VT: Jewish Lights Publishing.

Overeaters Anonymous, Inc. (1980). *Overeaters Anonymous.* New York.

Overeaters Anonymous, Inc. (1990). *The Twelve Steps of Overeaters Anonymous.* Torrance, CA.

Overeaters Anonymous, Inc. (1993). *The Twelve-Step Workbook of Overeaters Anonymous.* Torrance, CA.

Peck, M. Scott. (1978). *The Road Less Traveled.* New York: Simon and Schuster.

Progoff, Ira. (1975). *At a Journal Workshop.* New York: Dialogue House Library.

Seligman, Martin E. P. (1993). *What You Can Change and What You Can't.* New York: Knopf.

Sex and Love Addicts Anonymous. (1993). *Sex and Love Addicts Anonymous.* Boston, MA: Augustine Fellowship.

Simon, Sidney B., Leland W. Howe, and Howard Kirschenbaum. (1972). *Values Clarification.* New York: Hart.

Simon, Sidney B., and Suzanne Simon. (1990). *Forgiveness: How to Make Peace With Your Past and Get on with Your Life.* New York: Warner Books.

Taylor, Jeremy. (1983). *Dream Work.* Ramsey, NJ: Paulist Press.

Trimpey, Jack. (1994). *The Final Fix for Alcohol and Drug Dependence.* Lotus, CA: Lotus Press.

Trimpey, Jack, and Lois Trimpey. (1995). *Taming the Feast Beast.* New York: Delacorte Press.

Ury, William. (1991). *Getting Past No: Negotiating with Difficult People.* New York: Bantam.

Washton, Arnold, and Donna Boundy. (1989). *Willpower's Not Enough.* New York: HarperPerennial.

Weekes, Claire. (1972). *Peace from Nervous Suffering.* New York: Signet.

Wilt, Joy. (1979). *Handling Your Ups and Downs.* Columbus, OH: Weekly Reader Books.

World Service Office, Inc. (1987). *Narcotics Anonymous.* Van Nuys, CA.

Videotapes:

Berman, Marvin (Producer/Director). (1992). *MICA: MICARE Intervention Skills (Mental Illness/ Chemical Abuse Research and Education)*. Philadelphia, PA: MICARE.

WGBH. (1986). *Bodywatch: Relaxation Exercises*. WGBH, Boston, MA, 02134.